WITHDRAWN

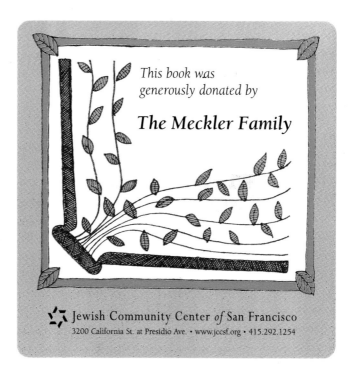

The Holocaust Odyssey
of
DANIEL BENNAHMIAS,

Sonderkommando

JUDAIC STUDIES SERIES

Leon J. Weinberger, General Editor

The Holocaust Odyssey
of
DANIEL BENNAHMIAS,

Sonderkommando

REBECCA CAMHI FROMER

With an Introduction by
Steven B. Bowman

The University of Alabama Press
Tuscaloosa and London

Library of Congress Cataloging-in-Publication Data

Fromer, Rebecca.
  The Holocaust odyssey of Daniel Bennahmias, Sonderkommando/
Rebecca Camhi Fromer : with an introduction by Steven B. Bowman.
    p.   cm.—(Judaic studies series)
  Includes bibliographical references and index.
  ISBN 0-8173-0598-X
    1. Auschwitz (Poland : Concentration camp)   2. Bennahmias, Daniel.
  3. Holocaust, Jewish (1939–1945)   4. Sonderkommandos.   5. Jews—
  Greece—Persecutions.   6. Greece—Ethnic relations.   I. Title.
  II. Series: Judaic studies series (Unnumbered)
D805.P7B424   1993
940.53' 18—dc20   92-25865

British Library Cataloguing-in-Publication Data available

Il mundo si esta quemando in braza biva,
y tu estas durmiendo endriva del buze.
—Sephardic proverb

The world is burning in a living flame,
and you sleep on ice.

Contents

Acknowledgments

I am indebted to Dr. Sybil Milton for a meticulous reading of the manuscript, to Dr. Steven Bowman for a lively collaboration on particulars, and to Ira Nowinski, Sybil Milton, and Sharon Camhi for making available to me the photographs that appear in this volume. I am further indebted to Max Garcia for bringing to my attention little-known details about the liberation of Ebensee and the brave stance of the *Ebenseer Fotoklub* in both confronting, researching, and recording the notorious history of the infamous camp in their midst. As a direct result of their efforts and kind permission, it has been possible to include a number of photographs that pertain to the story we have to tell.

I gratefully acknowledge my thanks to the Berliner Festspiele for permission to use a map detailing all the cities of origin of the transports to Auschwitz and to Yad Vashem for permission to use Erich Kulka's diagram of Birkenau, which first appeared under their copyright in *The Mills of Death: Auschwitz* by A. Krauss and E. Kulka in 1960.

To Alex Lauterbach and Fritz Hershberger for their generous help in translating passages in both Polish and German, and to René Molho for explaining the desperate attempts to ransom the Jews of Salonika and other dynamics, go my heartfelt thanks. The photocopy of the transports that entered Auschwitz from Greece was taken by a friend and given to me some years ago by Isaac Sevi.

The selflessness with which Daniel Bennahmias approached the telling of this most difficult story cannot be discounted. It has been an honor to work with him, as he worked on behalf of us all.

Introduction

The Greeks in Auschwitz

STEVEN BOWMAN

*I*n *The Holocaust Odyssey,* Rebecca Fromer leads us through the experiences of Danny Bennahmias, a Greek Jew of Italian citizenship whose forced labor as a Sonderkommando at Auschwitz included the disentangling of hundreds of thousands of gassed men, women, and children. The book is the result of a diligent collaboration. As it unfolds, it becomes a poignant reminder of the manner in which enslaved Jews and others were forced to destroy their families and fellow prisoners. It is a story of human decency, the spark of which remains against all odds.

Who were the Greek Jews? What was their fate? How did they contribute to the Auschwitz/Birkenau story, and what are the ramifications of the Sonderkommando revolt? As we proceed, we shall attempt to assay these and other questions.

◆　　◆　　◆　　◆

Greek Jews constituted a rich mosaic of Balkan and Aegean traditions and could recall historically several millennia of Hellenistic and Byzantine experiences. The vast majority of Jews in Greece, however, were exiles from Spain, or Sephardim. As such, they established, from the end of the fifteenth century onward, a unique center in Salonika that, by 1943, could look back proudly to over 450 years of life in the "Jerusalem of the Balkans," as they called their city. By that date, there were still some 50,000 Jews trapped in Salonika, overshadowed by the headquarters of Germany's Army Group E. In the spring of 1944, less than one-tenth of one percent of these Jews remained hidden in Salonika, while of those deported to Auschwitz, perhaps only three percent still survived.[1]

For several centuries, the Sephardi Jews had constituted the majority population in Salonika. Their residential areas surrounded the port, which was the major entrepôt for the Balkans. Their stevedores loaded and unloaded the ships that docked there. Their clerks, officials, and merchants predominated in the economic life of the region. Their schools and yeshivas trained generations of faithful Jews for the forty-odd synagogues of the city and rabbis for the Sephardi congregations of the Balkans and Jerusalem. Their many public and private libraries preserved the intellectual resources of half a millennium. And since the late nineteenth century, a vibrant secular culture had emerged that was to enrich the new nationalist movement of the Jews in the homeland of Zion. Even the Nazis, as their own records show, were impressed with the uniqueness of this great Jewry that they had conquered.

---

1. Cf. my entries in *The Encyclopedia of the Holocaust,* 1–4 (Macmillan, 1990), s.v. Greece, Salonika, Athens, Corfu, Rhodes, etc., for specific details and figures.

From the time of the German occupation of Salonika on April 9, 1941, following their entry into the Balkans to "assist" the Italian army—which the Greeks had trapped for some six months in the snows of Albania—some 5,000 Jews of Salonika had escaped to Athens or to the rural areas of the Italian-occupied zone of Greece. These were mostly the wealthy and the educated. They went into hiding in occupied Athens or in the villages and mountains of Free Greece, or they escaped to Turkey through the Resistance network. Only a few of these were caught in the roundups of communities throughout Central Greece during the Passover night of March 24–25, 1944, or during subsequent arrests in Athens. The Germans were assisted in these roundups by several Jewish traitors, including Pepo and Costa Recanati. Among the few Salonikans arrested were Danny Bennahmias and his family. Despite the heretofore loophole of their foreign nationality, they joined thousands of Greek Jewish citizens on the death trains. In the memoir itself, we shall read that the youthful Danny was unaware of the complicated diplomatic processes that Jews of Italian citizenship engendered for the politicians and the armies of the Axis.[2] Himmler himself wrote a testy letter to the Italians in March 1943, but to no avail; the Italians procrastinated to the very end of their involvement in the war.[3]

By the summer of 1944, Greek Jewry had been deci-

2. The story of the Greek Jew Errikos Sevillias has been published as *Athens-Auschwitz*, translated and introduced by Nikos Stavroulakis (Athens, 1983). Cf. Christopher Browning, *The Final Solution and the German Foreign Office: A Study of Referat DIII of Abteilung Deutschland 1940–43* (London and New York, 1978).

3. See now Jonathon Steinberg, *All or Nothing: The Axis and the Holocaust 1941–1943* (London and New York, 1990).

mated. Perhaps 10,000 Jews were in hiding in the mountains, in the villages of Free Greece under the protection of the Resistance, or in the occupied cities, especially Athens. Between 600 and 900 Jews were actually fighting in Resistance units, and many more were in the auxiliaries, whether as liaison with the British as interpreters, in various quartermaster functions, or as medical personnel (doctors and nurses). Also, many Greek Jews had escaped into Allied-controlled areas of the Mediterranean to fight with Greek and British forces against the Germans. Minos Levis, for example, was credited with saving the gold reserve of the Greek National Bank and smuggling it intact to the Greek government-in-exile in Cairo. Numerous others succeeded in reaching Palestine, where they were absorbed by their coreligionists. And about 65,000 had been deported to their deaths or enslavement in Eastern Europe.

In March 1943, the Bulgarians arrested the 4,000 Jews (nearly all of them Greek citizens) of occupied Thrace and sent them to Vienna, where Eichmann's organization directed them to Treblinka and the total annihilation of ninety-seven percent of the Sephardim of the northern Aegean littoral. Beginning in March 1943, Eichmann's emissaries Dieter Wisliceny and Alois Brunner directed the transfer—via nineteen or twenty trains from Salonika—of some 50,000 to the extermination center of Auschwitz. Eighty-five percent of these Jews, including all the aged, the infirm, the mothers, and the children (under twelve), were gassed on arrival. Italy left the war in September 1943, and on Passover, 1944, the Germans arrested the Jews of the former Italian-occupied zone of Greece. In June, the Jews of Corfu followed them to Auschwitz, and shortly thereafter, the Jews of Rhodes met the same fate. Out of all those deported, less than 2,000 survived the war and returned to Greece (see lists of transports in appendix).

When the Greek Jews first arrived at the Auschwitz railroad station, they had to march to the concentration camp, since the tracks had not yet been extended to the birch copse that would give its name to Birkenau. The young men who were selected during the spring of 1943 were responsible for building the barracks and crematoria of Birkenau and the factories of Monowitz/Buna, which were known respectively as Auschwitz II and Auschwitz III. The young women were sent into the swamps to drain them. Many received slight infections that, however, were sufficient to have them selected for the gas. Others were caught up in the periodic thinning of the camp ranks. Albert Menasche recalls in his memoir the selection of October 19–20, 1943, in which 2,500 girls were selected and three days later sent to the gas chambers. Among these girls were 800 from Salonika, including his daughter Lillian, who watched him play in the orchestra as she and his nieces were trucked away with the others.

The Jews who came from Greece were multilingual[4] and

4. The youths knew Greek and understood the Judeo-Spanish (popularly called Ladino) of their parents. Many had learned Italian, French, German, or English, depending on their secondary education. A few German Jews had intermarried with Salonikans, and some of these served as Kapos. Many knew Hebrew either from religious or Zionist training. A few knew Turkish or Bulgarian. What they did not know was Yiddish or East European Slavic tongues, and this has given rise in the literature to their ignorance of foreign languages, an assumption that does not stand the test of inquiry for many individuals, although as a general observation, it is a useful assumption (see author's note).

could be found throughout the levels of Auschwitz in its bureaucracy as secretaries and in its skilled labor force as carpenters, painters, engineers, etc. In addition, they could be found in its medical service, in its male and female orchestras, in its sporting events, and in most of its Kommandos, including the Canada, or sorting center. Interestingly enough, the Balkan middleweight boxing champion, a Greek Jew from Salonika, was undefeated in Auschwitz and therefore was not killed, as were his defeated opponents. Both the men and the women were singers of Greek dirges, while the men were a distinct presence in the last Sonderkommandos from Spring 1943 to Fall 1944.

Greek Jews could be found in the many work Kommandos outside of the Auschwitz system of thirty-nine subcamps, as well. Their odyssey took them to many of the main concentration camps and to the many labor camps, which their strong longshoremen and stevedores helped to build (and this story has yet to be chronicled in all its complexity), but nonetheless, it took a heavy toll of those selected for slave labor upon arrival at Auschwitz.[5] Many of the Greek Jews channeled into the subcamps never saw Auschwitz, for they had been drafted directly out of the quarantine. Of those who survived, many did not know of the destruction of their families until late in or even after the war.

In addition, it is known that a contingent of at least 1,000 Greek Jews became part of the history of the Warsaw ghetto from September 1943 to August 1944. Of these, less than 300 survived the death march from Warsaw to Dachau in July 1944. Between 100 and 200 others fought heroically in

5. Cf. Errikos Sevillias, *Athens-Auschwitz,* and Albert Menasche, *Birkenau (Auschwitz II)* (New York, 1947).

the Polish revolt that bloodied Warsaw in August 1944. Estimates are that fewer than thirty Greeks survived that fighting, many with distinction. Recent scholarship notes that Greeks fought bravely where and when they could. Indeed, as has been argued by Greek survivors, many young men and women would have fought in defense of their homeland and families had they been warned in time of the Nazi plan for their extermination.

The manifold complexities of the Greek experience are sure to be explored at length in further studies; here, however, we may delve into the Greek connection with the Sonderkommandos.

The policy at Auschwitz was to select a number of the strongest from the new arrivals to work in the crematoria. This process and the hazy notions surrounding the kind of work they would be required to perform are made very clear in Bennahmias's account. After indoctrination, which generally consisted of systematically imbibing varied alcoholic drinks and eating the "delicacies" from the supplies brought in by the intended victims (at least according to some of the reports), they were trained in their new tasks. Danny's experience constitutes a departure of sorts and, at the very least, indicates that the indoctrination procedure was more fluid than programmed. The previous Sonderkommando was culled very efficiently, sent to the gas chamber, and cremated—sometimes in Birkenau, but more often in the crematorium of Auschwitz I (at least the other prisoners thought as much). It is known in this connection that the victims were duped from time to time in order to keep a semblance of order and hope among the slaves who still remained in the Sonderkommando. Many of these victims knew, of course, of their imminent fate.

Of the several recorded stories of the Greeks in the

Sonderkommando, one is the unique report of some 400 men who were drafted for work but refused even after being informed that they would at once suffer the fate of their families in the gas chambers. The first reference to this unique incident in the annals of the camp appeared already in 1947 in Olga Lengyel's *Five Chimneys*. She dates the following incident to July 1944: "An extra shift of the Sonderkommando was added. (This was due to the influx of huge numbers of Hungarian Jews to the killing center.) Still it was not enough. At least four hundred Greeks from the Corfu and Athens transport were ordered in the Sonderkommando. Now, something truly unusual happened. These four hundred demonstrated that in spite of the barbed wire and the lash they were not slaves but human beings. With rare dignity, the Greeks refused to kill the Hungarians! They declared that they preferred to die themselves first. Sadly enough, they did. The Germans saw to that. But what a demonstration of courage and character these Greek peasants had given. A pity the world does not know more about them."

We learn more about the origin of these Jews from the Auschwitz records compiled by Danuta Czech of the museum located on the grounds of that killing center.[6] She records that a convoy of Greek Jews arrived from Athens on June 20 and consisted of 2,000 Jews, including approximately 1,795 from Corfu and the remainder from Athens and other Greek locales. Four hundred forty-six men and 131 women were selected for labor; the remainder, mostly from Corfu, were gassed. From Dr. Miklos Nyiszli, the

6. Danuta Czech, "Deportation und Vernichtung der griechischen Juden im K.L. Auschwitz," *Hefte von Auschwitz* 2(1970):5–37.

Hungarian prisoner who was responsible for performing the autopsies in the crematoria, we learn the following: "Last night they had burned the Greek Jews from the Mediterranean island of Corfu, one of the oldest communities of Europe. The victims were kept for twenty-seven days without food or water, first in launches, then in sealed box cars. When they arrived at Auschwitz's unloading platform, the doors were unlocked, but no one got out and lined up for inspection. Half of them were already dead, and the other half in a coma. The entire convoy, without exception, was sent to number two crematorium."[7]

Apart from the 400 Jews who had refused to live as Sonderkommandos, another act of open resistance involved the attempted escape of Alberto Errera, a career officer in the Greek army from Larissa, who was on a special Kommando that disposed of the victims' ashes in the nearby Vistula. While on assignment, Errera attacked one of the guards with his shovel, attempted to swim across the river, but was shot and recaptured.[8] Danny both knew and admired Alberto, as will be seen in the present account; however, according to another memoir, Errera's act had a significance beyond his own individual hope for success. In still another act of resistance, a Greek army captain attempted suicide, but he was revived by Dr. Nyiszli.

The revolt in Auschwitz, so important to the self-esteem of the prisoners at the time and so historically misconstrued, is a complex series of stories told on different levels

7. Miklos Nyiszli, *Auschwitz: A Doctor's Eyewitness Account* (New York, 1960).
8. Stavroulakis dates this incident between September 21 and 29, 1944 (*Athens-Auschwitz*, 103).

and from different perspectives. The Jews of Greece have distinctive contributions of their own to make to this unfolding tale; however, the predominant historiography of the revolt is by Polish Gentile and Polish Jewish survivors, hence the discrepancy between the majority of scholarship on the revolt and the role of the Greeks as recorded in their memoirs, as will be noted below. A careful reading of this material demonstrates that the Polish Jews were dependent for planning and implementation of the revolt on the Polish Gentile underground in the camp, which controlled access to and contact with the Polish Resistance in the woods surrounding the main camp.

The Polish Gentiles, who were the first prisoners in Auschwitz, were able to set up a sophisticated network that was able to smuggle individuals and information in and out of the camps; in addition, they were able to protect various persons deemed important to their mission of chronicling the atrocities and in preparing for the revenge they hoped to take when the Germans lost the war. To them, a physical revolt was considered to be an option only, one to be resorted to only in the case of a Nazi decision to annihilate the entire prisoner population. The Resistance in the forest was ancillary to this underground and acted as couriers; as such, they maintained contact with the main body in the camp. As long as the Nazis were preoccupied with killing Jews, however, the Polish Gentiles evinced no urgency to implement their plans for a revolt. It is therefore not surprising that several memoirs by Polish Jews consistently blame the Polish Gentiles not only for procrastination but also for the cancellation of the dates set for the revolt.

By August 1944, we pick up the testimony of Leon Cohen, a Sephardi Jew whom Danny knew and with whom he served as a Sonderkommando, as he attempts to chronicle subsequent events. According to Cohen, the ill treatment accorded to the Greeks in the Sonderkommando, and the shock of the horrible things they were made to do, had led them to conclude that the ovens had to be blown up as soon as possible: "We must not permit them to murder us like animals in a slaughter house." But they had no weapons, a lack that was not overcome until the revolt of September 7, 1944,[9] which Cohen specifically designates as the "revolt of the Jews from Greece," assisted by a dozen Russian soldiers and a handful of Jews.

Periodic additions were made to the Sonderkommando from the Hungarian transports. At regular intervals, these men were shipped out of Birkenau to other camps, allegedly Mauthausen, where they themselves were cremated. According to Cohen, this information, revealed by a German who was drunk at the time, shocked the prisoners who had accepted the official version, which claimed that the Hungarians had been transferred to work in another crematorium. At this point, the Greeks were convinced that certain death awaited them. This latter view is at variance with what both Daniel Bennahmias and Dario Gabbai have asserted, however, for they have made it clear that they knew death awaited them on two counts: the first, by virtue of their isolation from the other prisoners, and the second, by virtue of the very nature of the work they were com-

9. Postwar Greek reports date the revolt to September 1944, a discrepancy of one month that cannot be easily explained. This has led one scholar to claim mistakenly that there were actually two revolts. It may be that the Greek reports stem from one original report, to which their later memoirs refer or upon which they rely. The official date of the revolt is Saturday, October 7, 1944.

pelled to do. Still, there were examples to them of veterans of earlier Sonderkommandos who had survived periodic selections, such that some prisoners may have hoped for similar luck.

The Greek prisoners were in a special situation, denigrated by the Polish and other northern Ashkenazi Jews, who called them "cholera" and "korva" (whores). When Cohen complained to Koczak, the latter replied that the Ashkenazim were churls and boors who looked down on the Sephardim, avoiding them except when they wanted gold to trade. This animosity of Ashkenazim toward the Sephardim runs like a refrain through nearly all of the Greek memoirs, and it is certainly suggested by Danny.

The Sonderkommando began to organize resources for the revolt. Medicines were gathered from the victims of the never-ending transports. Each man set down his experiences, and then the document was buried in a glass bottle thirty centimeters below the courtyard of the crematoria.[10] Finally the date of August 15 was set, since that day coincided with the Feast Day of Saint Mary and the prisoners expected the guards to get drunk. Tension rose, and the prisoners scoured the transports for knives, sulfur tablets, and aspirin. Every night, the leaders went over their plans for the mass breakout. On August 10, Kapo Kaminsky made the rounds and warned the men to be cautious.

---

10. A number of these memoirs were subsequently found, and these form the basis for the reconstruction of events insofar as the particular writer was aware of the story (see following notes). This source material, while invaluable, has complicated the historical sequence of the revolt incidents. For example, Cohen's letter was found after the liberation of Auschwitz, and on the basis of it, his wife in Salonika received condolences from the Italian consul there. Relevent bibliography is listed in the articles cited in note 12 below.

On August 12, Auschwitz was shelled (by the Russians according to Cohen's later recollection; he appears here to be confusing the bombing of the camp by the Allies, since the Russians would not arrive at Auschwitz before January 1945). The prisoners were ecstatic. They were about to be liberated! The shelling ceased on the 13th, and rumors were rife. Kaminsky argued that the time was ripe to revolt and that they should not wait for the planned 15th holiday. With the cessation of the shelling, many of the Kommandos withdrew from the planned revolt. To many, the situation no longer seemed so hopeless. But the Russians (possibly the source for Cohen's mistaken identity of the attackers) in Crematorium I continued to plot.

The Greeks, according to Cohen, returned to thoughts of revolt after the cremation of the Hungarian and Belgian transports. Only the Russians, however, were keen on participating. After the events of the Errera incident, covered in the present text, the other prisoners demonstrated against the Greeks, calling them "cholera" and "bandits." But Errera had served to strengthen the Greek resolve, and the Russians saluted his brave deed, which they compared with the fate of their own comrades. Meanwhile, the Germans increased their guard and began to decimate the Sonderkommando. They assembled veteran prisoners to go to Mauthausen, or so everyone believed. Thus Crematoria II, III, and IV were reduced from their complement of 1,125. The Greeks realized that their turn was not far behind, and they determined to revolt.

The Greek sources for the Sonderkommando revolt are sparse indeed, Only eleven Greeks from the Sonderkommando survived the war, and fewer than 2,000 deportees returned to Greece after the war. Only one of the Sonderkommando memoirs has been published to date, that of

Leon Cohen, and it has not yet been subject to a critical reading by scholars.[11] Other Greek memoirs report on the Sonderkommando beginning with the 1947 memoir of Albert Menasche. His testimony is somewhat vague and is based on conversations with friends in Crematorium III and later memoirs. Interestingly enough, the memoir of Dr. Marco Nahon reports the testimony of a Sonderkommando slave, an Athenian Jew, but he does not mention the revolt at all. Sevillias, too, offers some comments on the incident in his memoir. Later researchers embellished Menasche's and others' accounts to enhance the Greek participation in the revolt. Danny's memory supplies another perspective on this incident, which has developed its own mythologies among the different ethnic groups that survived Auschwitz.

There are many points on which the accounts of Leon Cohen and Danny Bennahmias coincide in their recall of the events surrounding the revolt. What is important for the historian is to separate the various stages and levels of the revolt in any final assessment of this incident. Hence there was the overall camp plan for revolt that Joseph Garlinski explains in his books and articles. Next there is the tradition of Polish Jews, typified by the careful scholarship of Yisrael Gutman and Erich Kulka (both Auschwitz survivors), and summarized in many scholarly surveys. A number of Ashkenazi memoirs from surviving and dead Sonderkommando prisoners add other facets to the story. Finally, there is the Greek perspective told in repeated detail that suffers from occasional inaccuracies and partisan memory in the survey of Michael Molho and Joseph

11. In Hebrew translation from a French typescript prepared in the 1970s in *Pe'amim* 27 (1986).

Nehama's *In Memoriam* (first published in 1948) and in a number of poignant memoirs, e.g., Albert Menasche, Leon Cohen, and Danny Bennahmias.[12]

In retrospect, we may say that the revolt in Crematoria III and IV was a Greek-inspired riot, badly planned and doomed to failure. Its motto was Freedom in Death. The attempted escape of Crematorium I was discoordinated from the revised plan of August 15 for a mass camp revolt initiated by the entire Sonderkommando. There is more to be explored in terms of the leadership and organization of the Greeks and of their relationships with their Ashkenazi coreligionists. Researchers must give some pause to the general historiographic traditions that surround the complexities of that incident. It is hoped that future scholarship will take these points into consideration in order to arrive at a better understanding of what happened on that Sabbath that witnessed the final act of Greek Jewish martyrdom during the period we now call the Holocaust.

---

12. A preliminary bibliography is available in my "Jews in War-Time Greece," *Jewish Social Studies* 48 (Winter 1986):45–62. For references, see my "Jews in Wartime Greece: A Select Annotated Bibliography," in *Greece in the 1940s: A Bibliographic Companion*, edited by John O. Iatrides (University Press of New England, 1981), 83–94.

Author's Note

The account you are about to read unfolded over a period of three years, during which no tape recorders were used. Quoted materials are therefore distillations of the many discussions held. They are accurate representations, if not the precise words of what transpired.

Both Auschwitz I (Main Camp) and Auschwitz II (Birkenau) had crematoria; they operated at different times and had overlapping numerical designations. In this account, we will refer to the four crematoria in Birkenau as I, II, III, and IV; however, in some accounts, they appear as II–V. The crematorium in Auschwitz I is implied in this latter designation.

Unlike other prisoners, the Jews of Greece were unused to the severity of the winters of Eastern and Central Europe, and they suffered greatly on this account. In addition, they did not speak either Yiddish or German. They spoke French, Greek, Ladino (or Judeo-Spanish), and Italian, but these languages were not necessarily assets in the concentration camp. This last disadvantage served to limit their communication with both their overseers and their fellow prisoners. They therefore became a tightly knit unit, even as they experienced a kind of multiple of isolation.

Rebecca Fromer
Berkeley, California

The Holocaust Odyssey
of
DANIEL BENNAHMIAS,

Sonderkommando

Daniel Bennahmias
I. Nowinski

I

The Shock of Recognition

*You cannot imagine how terrible
Danny looked when he got home. I fed
him and I fed him. "Here, eat," I
said, and I fed him again. What
stories we told in those days!*
—Mary Rouben

We are friends, and we have talked about getting this story down for about a year. When we meet for the first time with this specific objective in mind, however, neither of us suspects how long it will take. We are in earnest as we begin, and Danny is the first to speak.

"One day, as I was on my way home from school—this was in Salonika—I ran into an old friend. After a while, he asked me if I had ever heard of Beethoven. I told him that I had not. 'Here, take this,' he said. Before I knew it, he had thrust a recording of Beethoven's Second Symphony into my hands. When I got home, I played it on our Victrola—

I'm sure you know the kind I mean—and I went wild. That day, I must have lost my mind and driven my mother crazy. I could not hear this music enough, and I played it over and over again. Beethoven was a discovery for me. Later on, when I was in Auschwitz—walking from crematorium I to crematorium II—I heard the first few bars of Beethoven's Fifth emanating out of a room occupied by a German officer. The door was ajar, and the radio was on. *Pom-pom-pom-pom; pom-pom-pom-pom; pom-pom-pom-pom.* . . . I convulsed violently and doubled over. In the galleys of hell, I had been reminded of a life that was no more and could never be again.

II

The Absence of Light

"My mother was afraid of death," said Danny. "She wasn't afraid of dying, you understand, but death itself was incomprehensible to her, and it terrified her. Perhaps she spoke to my father about how she felt—I do not know—but she never said anything to me. She did not have to, really. The signs of dread were unmistakable. For days after someone—anyone—died, she would not let the dark gain entry into the house. All night long, the lights burned, and not so much as a corner was allowed to remain unlighted or obscure. An incredible tension plunged us into an eerie reality in which it was light day or night—and that light became our beacon, so that death would not touch us or crash onto the little island we called home.

"My mother's ritual was both simple and highly idiosyncratic. The light kept vigil over us, and she kept vigil over it. She did nothing on account of any traditional notion or observance—we were not religious, in any case—nor did she set any pattern as to how long the lights might burn.

The object was to dispel the terror—and in time, I became convinced that the period of illumination was connected to and determined by her emotional state. Now, what impressed me about this phenomenon of my mother's was that when an uncle of mine who lived in Paris died, we once more were treated to the light in this singular fashion. This was extraordinary to me.

"What I cannot get out of my mind, and what it is impossible for me to understand, is what happened when we were being deported from Athens to Auschwitz. You see, when we were packed into boxcars, everything was done so 'correctly,' as to seem natural. A formula had been devised, which allowed atrocity the play of a devastating norm.

"We were crammed into the boxcars, and that was that. We no longer mattered to anyone. We were sealed within steel—a thicket of people so densely packed that even as the strands of our life disintegrated, we knit together and formed a tortured human web within which we were virtually locked into place. When one moved, we all moved. There was no other way.

"Most of us overcame enormous inhibitions in those terrible days—it could not have been otherwise—and yet the strange thing is that I cannot remember what we did, or how we took care of ourselves. Have I blocked everything out? Is that it? Certainly. Do not ask me if there were slop pails aboard the train, or any details of that sort; there were none to my recollection.[1] Do not ask me if there were conversations or quarrels, love making, tears, screams, wild laughter. It is all gone. What has stayed with me is of an

---

1. He later remembered that there was a big pail for their needs and that it was a mess.

entirely different order. We had no food and no water, and
the train never stopped so that we could relieve ourselves.

"We were young and old; men, women, and children.
There was modesty among us. Respect. I think you can
understand. We had come from an entirely different world
than the one into which we had been thrust. What were
we to do now? How were we to behave? How could we
behave? The exercise of choice is the option of free men,
and we were not free. We were mothers and daughters,
fathers and sons; we had to deal with the pregnant, the
infant, the aged, and every manner of natural occurrence—
whether it was menses, a heart attack, or anything else that
might arise—and what is more, we had to deal with a full
range of intelligence from the precocious to the naive. How
did we do it? What did we do? Those of us who did not
perish managed everything somehow, but for the life of me,
I don't know how it was done.

"Dire as our situation was, we little realized what awaited
us. Oh yes, we had heard of the *trains de la mort,* but their
significance eluded us entirely. The BBC made elliptical
references to work in the east, or forced labor, and even
mentioned the death trains, but it never established a clear
connection between the two—and so we thought, ah well,
this is how the British use figurative language. We will 'die'
of exhaustion: this is what they mean. None of us could
conjure visions of the actual significance of what lay behind
either the innuendos or a series of thinly shrouded events,
but today, it seems incredible to me that we did not have the
slightest idea of what would happen to us. Now, had the
British been explicit, would we have believed them? In all
fairness, I do not think so. The horror of an unthinkable,
unpronounceable truth would have been suppressed or

dismissed as baseless propaganda or a cruel hoax. Still, why didn't they say the Germans gassed people? Why didn't they say there was a Sobibor or a Treblinka? Why weren't we given the chance to be 'crazy enough' to believe them? Why? What harm would it have done? And so, you see, we found ourselves in the situation we were in because we did not know what we now know.

"Our suffering mounted and wore on into the ninth day of a wearying, fearfully lonely journey, and ever since then, I have tried to find the words to express what we went through. I don't know what they are. I can't discover them. Whatever I do, however I try, I fall short of it; my mind goes blank—but if this language is not available to me, who knows if it exists?

"Now, it so happened that the woman who sat next to my mother in the boxcar died positioned across my mother's chest, where her body remained rigidly in place for two days. My mother froze in absolute terror; she averted her head and neither moved nor spoke again. Two entire days—the last two days of her life—were spent in this way. The corpse lay in her lap and putrefied there. No one could do anything; no one could say anything. I looked at my mother, and my father looked at my mother. That was all. We were helpless. The death my mother so feared was beginning to overtake her.

III

The Unfolding Debacle

"With the breakup of the Turkish Empire in 1912, we were confronted with the choice of either becoming Greek or registering as foreign nationals of Italian descent. The territory in which we now lived came under the jurisdiction of Greece, and we, who had family ties in Italy, had the opportunity of taking one course or the other. As it so happened, we could trace our heritage from Spain to some degree. We therefore did not rescind the Italian citizenship we had been entitled to for 150 or 200 years, as a result of having settled in Livorno at some time after the Inquisition.

"Everyone in our rather large family decided to become Greek for the sake of convenience, but my father, who felt this close connection to Italy, consolidated our citizenship accordingly. Now, as it turned out, the Jews of Greece fell into three categories: those who had managed to maintain their Spanish citizenship intact over the centuries—a privileged class which went to Bergen-Belsen rather than to Auschwitz—those who chose to become Greek, and those who, like us, became Italian. During the war, however, our national identities played a limited role. In effect, all 'categories' were pretexts—or conventions to be exploited at will. We were all meant to die, regardless of origin or affiliation. The records are clear on this point, inasmuch as more than ninety percent of the Jews of Greece were slaughtered one way or another.

"As a boy, I went to the Italian school, where I first learned Italian. I of course knew Greek and had absorbed Ladino, but at home we spoke French. At any rate, from time to time, it was considered 'ornamental' to dress after the Fascist style—I only wore my uniform once—and I sang songs that made my father laugh or wink mischievously at me when he heard them. My father applied for an annual work permit, and he confronted the nuisance of undergoing bureaucratic scrutiny year after year, which the rest of the family had taken into consideration and wished to avoid—but on the whole, everything was fine, life went on, and that was that. There were valid, if not compelling, reasons for the decisions we made in those days, and everyone was content. We had yet to discover that under the Germans—at least for a little while—we Italians were to receive preferential treatment over the Greeks.

"The Germans occupied Salonika, but farther south, in Athens, the Italians were in charge. There was a world of difference between the two forces, and it soon became apparent that as Italian Jews we complicated the German psyche. On the one hand, they had to contend with us as citizens of a friendly power—and on the other hand, their style was neither one of finesse, nor was their agenda friendly where we were concerned.

"The German occupation of Salonika was rather low-key

at first. There was a military presence, particularly in the
main sections of town, but no one made too much of this—
and in any case, it was more or less expected that an
occupying force would plunder, entrench itself, or otherwise
assert its authority.[1] When shops, offices, and homes were
confiscated, we saw the appropriation of the best of everything—and when the ghetto was instituted as late as March
25, 1943, we were not unduly alarmed, even though, by now,
the Greek Jews had to wear a yellow star. An inherent
ambiguity in German policy lulled us to our danger—and
although we may never know if what happened was the
result of flawed vision or genius, chance or design, in
retrospect, it is easy to see the simplicity with which the
sinister aspects of that policy were couched in the trappings
of safety. You see, the experience of the Jews of Greece
differed from that of other Jews elsewhere, in that when
they were concentrated into ghettoized areas, they lived
among non-Jews who were allowed to remain where they
were. This acted as balm, and it counterbalanced a good
many of the anxieties of disruption and upheaval. We did
not make light of events; it was not easy to be dispossessed

1. Despite Danny's calm assessment, both harassment and collu-
sion with the Gestapo were reported. Various agencies of the Jewish
community were subjected to incessant barrages of ominous calls
announcing imminent catastrophe or "so-called orders of the most
fantastic and ridiculous nature. . . ." And "Sometimes officers, inspired by malevolent local people, commit excesses against isolated
Jews. One notices every day cases of blackmailing . . . threatening to
denounce them as communists, or having their merchandise, homes,
and furniture confiscated. . . ." Quoted from Michael Molho, *In
Memoriam: Hommage aux Victimes Juives des Nazis en Grèce* (Thes-
salonique, 1973), 57 (relevant passages translated from the French by
Nelda Cassuto).

or dislocated—it was not pleasant by any means—but we rationalized that this was war, and we thought we knew what that was. We faced many hardships, including the deprivation of work, but we took our calamities in stride and tried to alleviate what suffering we could. Within six months, the Jewish community would have its hands full feeding the hungry, caring for the sick, and burying the dead, who lay in the streets where they fell and remained unclaimed. To have done otherwise would have required forfeiture of the deceased's ration card and virtually assured the perpetuation of death by starvation.

"Rumors about 'work in the east' trickled into consciousness some time before the creation of the ghetto. On Saturday, July 11, 1942, all male Jews between the ages of eighteen and forty-five were asked to report to Liberty Square.[2] The general assumption was that information would be forthcoming on the subject, which up until then had remained quite vague. You must understand that the proclamation or decree—or whatever it was—applied to all Jews of Greek descent and that my father and I were exempt as Italians.

"It was an extraordinarily hot day, and what ensued was as baffling as it was barbaric. All of my uncles, cousins, friends, and neighbors showed up among the swelling ranks that filled the square; the young and not-so-young and the strong and weak came from everywhere, eager for news. That day, 9,000 men in all presented themselves. Nine thousand! The Jews simply showed up—suspecting no ill

2. A communique to this effect appeared in *l'Apoghevmatini*, the Greek daily, which came out in the afternoons. Also refer to Molho, *In Memoriam*, 58.

and harboring neither thoughts nor fears of violence. This was to be our first lesson, you see, but no one understood the language of systematic humiliation or its link with annihilation at that time.

"From eight in the morning until two in the afternoon, the men who gathered were made to do 'sports' under the broiling sun of an oppressively humid day. Before long, they collapsed in the unprotected, unshaded square—with neither food nor water nor facilities to aid them in their distress—but when they dropped, they were set upon and beaten. They were bruised, kicked about, stomped on, maimed, or killed by the Germans, who were armed with machine guns.[3] No one dared to stop this brutal exercise, and when it was over, everyone went home having learned nothing more substantial than what it feels like to be the subject of a peculiar oppression and fixation.

"That evening it was very quiet. Friends and family embraced one another in silence. None had need of words, and in any case, words are not the sole bearers of intelligence. We were capable of reading a thought in the set of

3. "All around the square, machine guns and cannon of a small calibre are placed in a very visible way, crowning the tops of the buildings . . ." (Molho, *In Memoriam*, 58). Also see John A. Katris, *Eyewitness in Greece: The Colonels Come to Power* (St. Louis, 1971), 81: "While the registration was going on SS soldiers moved among the crowd with huge ferocious police dogs and amused themselves by various abuses. They ordered the Jews to disrobe and forced groups of them to do exercises or to dance. When someone fainted from overheating or exhaustion they poured buckets of water on him and forced him to continue. Others were made to roll like barrels, naked, all around the square. And now and again the Germans released the dogs to tear at the naked bodies on the ground."

the eyes, the slump of a shoulder, an involuntary shrug, or the nod of a disbelieving head. There was no need for tea leaf or coffee grain divination, and there was no need for gypsy cards or a crystal ball. We may not have known our murderers, but we certainly knew one another. And now, I suppose you would like to know what the men thought."

"Yes, I would, Danny."

"They thought the Germans were crazy."

"That's it?"

"Yes, that's it. Are you disappointed?"

Danny continued. "The episode seemed stupid, the circumstances too bizarre. For all we knew, someone had exceeded his authority or misunderstood the use of power. None of us saw it for what it was, you see—a stroke of genius in the negative art of social conditioning."

"Wasn't anyone critical of what had happened?" I asked.

"This worries you, I know, but just think for a moment. Isn't it true that if you believe someone is really mad, the most you will do is raise an eyebrow? Isn't it impossible to criticize anyone who is beyond the reach of reason? And in any case, what recourse do you imagine we had?"

I did not know, but I was troubled. "Didn't anyone want to leave—to get out—to escape—to organize—to defend? For God's sake, Danny, wasn't there anyone like that?"

"No, there wasn't. Well, that isn't quite right. A few had joined the Andartes, a rebel band in the hills, but they were the exceptions—individualists, idealists, and activists—for whom the perfect fusion of ideology and drama instilled the will to champion a cause. The rest of us had a difficulty with horror. We shut it out. We preserved our sanity at the cost of safety."

"Danny?"

"Yes?"

"As Italians, you and your father were spared the tyranny of that day in the square, but the rest of the family went; they were Greek, and they were there. The rigor and the humiliation fell to them, but didn't they resent this exclusion of yours?"

"No. They were happy we had been spared."

"Is that true, Danny?"

"Yes," he nodded. "You seem surprised."

In that moment, I realized that I was surprised. How can one think, I wondered. How should one think after the mirror of civilization shatters?

"Shall we go on?" asked Danny.

"Ummuh . . ."

"Very well then. On July 13, 1942,[4] just two days after the episode in Liberty Square, the Jewish Community Council—functioning under the order of the Germans[5]—

4. The twelfth, a Sunday, was not used for conscription. Salonika observed its Sundays, and little more than the cafés were open. There was no disruption of this practice on the part of the Germans.

5. The legal council, elected by the Jews of Salonika, was dissolved by the Germans, and its members were imprisoned for one or two days afterward. In their place, the Nazis chose Sabbatai Saltiel and a fellow by the name of Albala (a "Quisling") as their main spokesmen and implementors. Undaunted, the legitimate council held meetings in one another's homes to see how best to help the community and, if possible, to divert the collaborators from their disastrous course. Dr. Zvi Koretz, Viennese by birth, had functioned as the chief rabbi of Salonika but was made head of the community by the Germans. According to René Molho, whose father, Mario Molho, was a member of the legitimate council, Koretz was a "learned, naive, and stupid

issued a call for all young Jewish males of Greek nationality to report for labor in Greece.[6] Thousands came forward according to the lists on record with the council and were assigned work in either the fields or swamps. This work, supervised by the council, was on a minor scale; that is to say, it could not be compared to the magnitude of the transports. The men left for 'work' on buses or trams, came home on periodic leave, and received no compensation.

"Before long, it became evident that the men were not fed adequately, and the council—desperately busy in the city—now tried to assume the responsibility for sending food out to them.[7] This plan, however well intentioned, was doomed to failure because of food shortages and other complications. You see, the men on the work battalions contracted malaria, typhoid, and tuberculosis, and they had to be cared for. Now, there was a short supply of medical equipment—and antibiotics were almost impossible to obtain—but the situation grew hopeless as more and more men became stricken. Few men actually survived the work battalions, and within six months or so, it was quite apparent that they had been programmed for death.

---

man." Saltiel was "prone to self-importance and did not grasp the situation," and Albala collaborated "from a position of awareness." René Molho now resides in Oakland, California, and it was there that he conveyed the above to me.

6. Molho, *In Memoriam*, 60. More than 1,000 do not answer the call.

7. That is to say, the former, legitimate council, who worked on the sidelines, continued to maintain contact with the Jews of Salonika. As elected representatives, they had served as volunteers; as "deposed" councilmen, they did not do less. Information provided by René Molho.

"In February 1943, a Dr. Merten and a Dr. Wisliceny[8] approached the Jewish council with a proposal to end the work battalions. The Germans stipulated as a precondition, receipt of 250,000 gold francs, or Napoleoni, as they were sometimes called. Functioning under the pressure of time—and frantic to save those they could—the aroused community met the conditions of extortion set by the SS,[9] little realizing that the notorious transports were about to begin. In this manner, a little joke had been played upon the Jews, who had no way of knowing that death alone would deliver them from enforced labor.[10]

8. Kriegsverwaltungsrat Merten was the war administration counsellor with the commander of the Armed Forces in the Salonika-Aegean theater, and Hauptsturmführer Dieter Wisliceny was an SS captain representing the military administration in the Central Office. Both were instrumental in the deportation of the Jews of Greece; however, Wisliceny served as Eichmann's assistant. He was an SS expert.

9. The demand was made of Saltiel and Albala, but it was the legitimate council that marshalled itself into action and actually produced the ransom. During the transfer of funds, those present included Saltiel and Albala, the legitimate council, and Wisliceny and Merten. At this time, neither Wisliceny nor Merten addressed Saltiel or Albala, whom they had installed as their surrogates, but rather the legitimate council, to whom they had turned. René Molho learned of this from his father, who was present, and recounted the story to me.

10. After the war, Merten and Wisliceny were brought to trial. Merten's case ran a particularly convoluted course, and he was tried twice—once in absentia, and once after having been apprehended while on vacation in Thessaloniki (1959–60). Although found guilty in each instance, Merten was pardoned. Foremost among the crimes charged to him were those connected with the extermination of the Jews of the Thessaloniki area, but intervention on his behalf from Bonn, from Queen Frederika—who did not decline to wear her Nazi

uniform during the occupation or acknowledge her membership in the Hitler Youth Movement—and from highly placed officials in the Greek government, with whom he had collaborated, succeeded in stressing Greek-German friendship over the atrocities of the war (Katris, *Eyewitness in Greece,* 80–86).

Dieter Wisliceny: Born in Regulowken, East Prussia, 1911; studied theology; joined the Nazi party in 1931 and the SS in 1934; member of the Eichmann office in the Central Office for Reich Security (RSHA); responsible for the deportation of Jews from Slovakia, 1942, Greece, 1943–44, and Hungary, 1944; witness for the prosecution at Nuremberg; sentenced to death and executed in Czechoslovakia, 1948.

IV

The First Incarcerations

"Although my father and I enjoyed a certain immunity at the time of these events, we were not always spectators, nor would we remain so. For a little while, we were subject to a different aspect of the unfolding saga, and that is all. When the others had respite, we did not; when they did not, we did. This is how it went.

"Italy declared war on Greece on October 28, 1940; immediately afterward, we found ourselves cast into the mold of 'enemies of the state.' Within days, therefore, we became prisoners of the Greeks and entered into a unique reality—along with other Italians, Jew and non-Jew alike. We were now at the start of a curious odyssey that spanned the months between November 1940 and April 1941, at which time we were liberated by the Germans as 'allies.' In the end, of course, it did not matter whose nationals we were.

"Soon following the declaration of war, a summons went out for Italian men sixteen years of age and older to report to the former tobacco-processing plant in Salonika. Women and children were to stay at home, but we gathered our things, took such provisions as we could carry against the misfortunes of war, and presented ourselves at the appointed time.

"The day we surrendered ourselves was routinely uneventful. We were fed and treated decently, and in the evening, we were each given a blanket, which we could use as we wished. No cots had been provided, and we were to sleep on the floor. In the morning, we were on the move. Our destination was Argos, where we stayed for two or three days in a similarly uneventful manner. There, we were detained under a system that was more or less informal—a kind of guardianship—which allowed my father and me time together.

"From Argos we were taken to Maroussi, where we stayed at the Park Hotel for about five months. We lived comfortably, ate decently, and were subject to few restrictions. We could have visitors, write and receive letters, and go in and out of the hotel almost at will. Our guards were amiable, thoroughly decent Greeks, with whom we sometimes played cards—and because they were at ease with their humanity, they helped us whenever they could. If on occasion we felt like having a special treat—a change of diet, a departure from 'institutional food,' for example— they obliged us. We paid, and we shared—but what mattered most was how humanly accessible and responsive they were to us as people. To be honest with you, there seemed little reason for us to have been there at all.

"Our next stop was Athens, where the Germans 'liberated' us from the Greeks after our first week there. In another week, we would return to Salonika, but while we were in Athens, the situation was so relaxed that one day I saw an Italian soldier strolling in the street with about fifty or sixty Greeks in tow. The soldier, whose gun rested at his side, was besieged by requests. The men had sighted a kiosk that sold cigarettes, which they wanted to buy, but when the soldier refused, the men pressured him until he relented. Off they went as he sat on the curb, smoked a cigarette of his own, and waited until they reassembled at leisure. In the years to come, I would remember this scene because it was so markedly different from the treatment accorded us by the Germans.

"My mother's hair had turned completely gray in our absence. We had been gone six months. For two years—from 1941 through 1943—we lived in relative safety. I went back to my Italian school and played with my friends; my father immersed himself in work, and my mother continued to use the light to ward off death. The plague stored its strength and accelerated its virulence, and with no news of the outside world filtering our borders, the German forces grew and consolidated their hold over the land. They were seen everywhere as they strolled the avenues with their comrades and girlfriends, or as they talked to shopkeepers about the ordinary things of life.

"Little by little, however, the Italians began to encourage us to leave. It was all done very quietly, but by this time practically all of the Salonika transports had left. Captain Merci, the military attaché at the Italian Consulate, who helped the Jews even as he might have helped others in similar circumstances, issued at least fifty to sixty blank passports to my knowledge. Among those who received such passports were my grandmother, my cousin, and my aunt and uncle, all of whom went to Palestine. Emil Neri, who had no official post but who was a member of the

Fascist Party, also helped us enormously by serving as an intermediary. It was he who arranged for temporary safe houses and monies for the security of the people. Both were trusted, and neither acted from motives of personal gain. Most of the Italian Jews in Salonika acted as we did; they began to leave for Athens. The Italian presence there held greater sway and was more reassuring; the atmosphere was freer.

"We packed three or four suitcases to take along with us before we boarded the all-Italian train called the *Tradotta*. All of our other belongings remained in our rented house, entrusted to my mother's close friend, Mrs. Kiriakopoulou. The one and only time I returned to Salonika after the war, I looked in on her. She had kept everything intact, and I gave it all to her—all, that is, with the exception of the pens each of my parents wrote with. These I have and treasure to this very day.

"At any rate, when we arrived in Athens, it was not necessary to hide, and we rented a two-and-a-half-room apartment from a woman who had lost her husband in the mountains. He was an Andartis. We stayed with her until Italy capitulated in September of 1943.

"The Germans issued orders for the Jews to register in the Jewish Community House. Very few registered. We went underground, so to speak. We hid in the home of a lawyer acquaintance of my father, a Mr. Kristotakis. Of course, you understand, we did not register. We remembered what it was like in Liberty Square.

"Five of us then lived with the Kristotakises: my aunt and uncle, Rachel and Eli, my father and mother, and I. We basically lived in one room, but we were not confined to it and could circulate around the house. My father and uncle arranged for our meals to be brought in, and I remember that all of us ate in our one room. Since we had many friends in Athens, they came to visit us at night. We passed the time together in the room. Our neighbors knew we were there, but they constituted no threat.

"Concerned with their children's safety, my Aunt Rachel and Uncle Eli placed my cousins Jenny and Albert elsewhere. They were in the household of one called Fotinelli. This Fotinelli knew where we were and would come to us at regular intervals, for my aunt and uncle paid for their children's upkeep on a regular basis, even as we paid for ours at the Kristotakises. Jenny was fifteen at the time, and Albert was three or three and a half.

"While in hiding, I had a clandestine affair with the Kristotakises' daughter, which in time was detected. Although delicate, the situation was resolved without endangering the family—however, we were soon in a lot of trouble. When the threat finally came, you see, it was at the hands of a collaborationist, a Greek Jew by the name of Recanati, who had recognized Jenny as she sat on a park bench and had reported her to the Germans.

"As luck would have it, the very day that the Germans came for Jenny, Albert had been placed elsewhere, in a home better equipped to handle the needs of a three-year-old. Thus, when Jenny entered the German's vehicle and found someone else within it who had been rounded up, she sighed in relief: '*Gracias al dio, qui no toparon a mi hermano.*' 'Thank God, they haven't found my brother,' she said, but Recanati was right there, in the front seat of the jeep; he had overheard her and reported this, too, to the Germans. After that, it was only a matter of time before pressure was put upon Fotinelli to reveal Albert's whereabouts. With

Albert in hand, the Germans then returned to Fotinelli, demanding the location of the parents. There was no way for the poor man to avoid telling them what they wanted to know.

"On or about March 1st, at approximately 11:30 p.m., the Germans came for us. I was in my robe, but I was not allowed to dress. My Aunt Rachel asked my mother for her slip—or rather, she tried—but she had gotten badly frightened by the invading Germans, and from that point on, she stammered, unable to complete a thought. All our goods remained behind.

"The five of us were taken into downtown Athens to the Gestapo Interrogation Center in the Merlin Building, where we were locked into a long bathroom. The next day, I was called in for questioning. The interrogating officer, 'convinced' that I spoke German, jammed his fists into my face until I bled. He laughed and said: 'Come on, I know you speak German.' But I truly could not do the impossible. I knew no German, and so an interpreter was brought into the picture. 'We will let you go free,' they said, 'if you will tell us where the others are hidden.' This sort of thing went on for about thirty minutes, after which I was brought back to the bathroom. We stayed there for perhaps two days in all, and then we were taken to our first concentration camp in the town of Haidari. It was very large and was divided in two sections—one for the women and children, and another for the men. From where we were, we could see the women and children in the distance.

"The camp was run by a man named Napoleon Sougioultzidis, an individual who participated in the Resistance as an Andartis and was a prisoner himself. On two separate occasions, this Napoleon acted as my mother's emissary, and out of decency, he brought us the bread she wished to share with us from out of her own rations.

"The Germans devised various 'sports' for us, and I was put to digging. My father, however, had to haul a wheelbarrow filled with cement. He was kicked and taunted by a German, who followed him at his heels. 'Come on, go faster,' he would say, and then the blows fell. This angered me greatly. Insofar as I know, the women were not given such treatment.

"Once, in passing, a German officer saw my wristwatch. 'Oh, that is pretty,' he said, and with that, he put the watch on his own wrist and kept on walking. . . . What else can I say? There were about 300 men in Haidari. We knew some, and we got to know others—my friend Marcel Nadjari was there, for instance. We didn't socialize. At the time, we thought the place was awful. Then, on April 2nd, about a month after we had arrived, we were put on the transport for Auschwitz."

V

The Withdrawal

onths go by. We do not
meet. We make plans, but there are excuses. The year
erodes, and it is springtime. It is a struggle to stand still,
and it is a struggle to go forward. Everything set down thus
far is part of something larger we wish to convey, and yet
the pain of going ahead, along with the ordinary intrusions
of life, conspire against us.

Danny plans a vacation to Switzerland and Greece. He
does not feel as well as he would like, but he is enthusiastic
about going to Switzerland for the first time. I share with
him the little I know of Zurich, Einleiden, and Lucerne, and
later on, I drop in on him spontaneously in order to wish
him a good journey. I, who love opera, know that Danny
does not care for it, but it pleases me to tease him a little
with a disc containing the arias of Puccini heroines. "Here," I
say. "Your musical education is not over yet." "I know it
isn't," he says pleasantly, but Mary Rouben,[1] who is pres-

---

1. Mary was related to Danny by marriage. She and her husband,
Sam—along with several others—were rescued by Emil Neri as they
fled the ghetto in Salonika. They remained in hiding in Athens, not far

ent, remarks, "But he doesn't like opera!" "That's why she brought it," Danny responds, and we burst into laughter. Within seconds, however, we are treated to the first aria, and now it is I who am surprised. Danny not only knows the lyrics, but also sings along with the soprano:

> *Si, mi chiamano Mimi,*
> *ma il mio nome é Lucia.*
> *La storia mia é breve.*
> *A tela o a seta ricamo*
> *in casa e fuori.*
> *Son tranquilla e lieta*
> *ed é mio svago far gigli*
> *e rose. . . .*

"My father loved opera," he says. "I grew up with this."

During Danny's absence, I receive a letter from the director of the museum at Oswiecim. He has heard from a source in Israel that Danny and I are working together. They would like to have his story for their records. I tell them what I must. So far our data are not germane. What they want to know has been skirted and no more, but I will send what I have if that is what they want. Meanwhile, I learn what an Oswiecim postmark can do to me. It is a valuable lesson.

For two days I do not open the envelope. Its innocence appalls me. It becomes a dreadful specter precisely because it seems so innocuous, and now I have a problem. I do not know where to keep this letter. Wherever it lies, it disturbs

---

from the Kristotakis household, until the end of the war—and did not learn of this coincidence until then.

me. It repels me, but I cannot discard it. I wish it had never arrived, and I have trouble understanding why anyone from this infamous factory of death would write to me.

In the end, the letter creates an impact of another sort, a positive one. Can the museum have so little on hand that it takes an interest in what we do? Yes. Obviously. Records have been destroyed, and witnesses have been killed. Danny managed to survive against all odds, as did Dario, his lifelong friend. They are two of perhaps no more than a half-dozen or so men from the Sonderkommando to have been spared by fate. If their story is not told, it will be lost for all time. I feel I must proceed. If it means submitting an incomplete account, at least it will be as full as I can make it.

◆　◆　◆　◆

Danny remembered no facilities other than a big pail[2] aboard the transport because there were none. He and the others, all Jews, were herded onto the waiting cars with practiced disregard and made to endure an insufferable assault upon the sensibilities that most of us think of and recognize as civilized behavior and take for granted. Is it any wonder then that what stays most with Danny is his sense of impotence at his father's suffering and his mother's terror? The urine, the feces, the sloshing wastes evaporating into a noxious stench, lice, lack of sanitation, privacy, oxygen, water, food—that spectacle is repressed or contained, like encapsulated tubercular bacilli that no longer can do systemic harm.

There is no lexicon other than in the arts to address

2. Because of the trauma of the transport, Danny is actually unsure if it was a big pail or a small barrel.

the horror they knew—no other vocabulary to enrich our understanding of their dismay or disbelief—and no possible way to describe the battle waged between hope and fear on the doomed train in the abandonment of the sealed car, where even silence was electric with eloquence. The pretext of *the showers* was an utterly pacifying, believable ploy to be anticipated with some relief by the wearied victims, but who can depict the cynical deceptions and the denouement, in print or otherwise, with absolute fidelity? The consummate indignity of the gas chamber? Scrambling for air? Clutching for space, a child, and the absent God? The act of being crushed, and unwittingly crushing, too? Dying, fouled by a sorry plague of bladders and bowels and blood gone wild? Unprivate, and without the last grace? The depths of anguish cannot be plumbed; not now, not ever. Not in this case.

The transports' grueling purpose was to subdue, humiliate, and disorient those about to be killed[3] by means of the

---

3. If the ramifications of this point are not understood fully, one cannot comprehend how thousands upon thousands went into "the showers" uncomplainingly. Danny makes it quite clear that he never heard anyone cry, scream, panic, protest, or otherwise rebel when entering the gas chamber. They had been conditioned for death, even as they had been conditioned for a shower. These two factors were the inextricable, simultaneously evolved dynamics of their ordeal. According to him and others, however, there were differences to be noted among those who were already in the camp. When selections were made from within their ranks, one did hear cries from time to time. Such cries, when they occurred, were not defiant but, rather, passive—a kind of "letting go" of the illusion that they might have lived. Once, Danny heard these Jews and their lamentations from a distance, but this must have been before the chamber door had been closed. Because Danny's statement may seem to contradict what is some-

crudest, most efficient means available; that is to say, the victims were to be rendered helpless by subterfuge—*labor in the east*—and by an awesome isolation compounded by practices designed to dehumanize. The victimizers, having learned the lessons of the past, however, were to be as insulated as possible from harmful psychological or emotional trauma. The Jews, treated as nonentities and viewed as disposable goods or things, were either to be devoured by the machine or to be used by it and then devoured. The business of the transport was death—not work—and the business of the camp was death—not work. Death was not to be kind, and work was to be an instrument for death.

The employment of sociopathic or criminal elements in key positions would ensure a high toleration for atrocity and intrigue, but the bureaucratic, methodological requirements of the German mind imposed order to levels of unreason and acceptable madness—and this, too, became part of the design for death. The union between the refinements of sadism and standard procedures for annihilation as a policy of state were to live side by side, and each was to give rise to a distinctive brand of intimidation and terror. None but those put to death immediately was to escape the fullest possible understanding of this grotesque

---

times said about these matters, it is critical to remind the reader that there were five crematoria, two bunkers, and numerous vast pits into which children and adults sometimes were thrown while still alive. Birkenau's Crematoria I and II were the most efficient and best insulated of all the crematoria, and Danny recounts that once he went right past the window of an already filled chamber. He saw the crush of people and some who seemed to be beseeching the divinity, but he heard nothing.

encampment—and they had paid the ultimate price for the recognition that was theirs before oblivion.

The minutes, hours, and days of Danny's transport were inhumanely savage times that came to an end on April 11, 1944,[4] nine days after his having left from Athens. Within twenty-five or thirty minutes of arrival at the selection platform, those unknowingly reprieved from certain death had been culled out from the multitude about to die within the next hour or two. A special ramp, being built expressly for the purpose of handling people in greater numbers more expeditiously, would be in operation before long. Under the new system, the unsuspecting souls would be made to take a five- or six-minute walk to the killing center, where they faced immediate extinction; under this system, however, trucks were used to move the intended victims from the platform to the killing center a half-mile outside of Birkenau. The functioning chimneys and the fifteen high-speed ventilators that were already fanning the crematoria fires awaited them. Danny's mother and father were among the 1,067 persons to die in the crematoria from this transport alone. Three hundred twenty men and 113 women survived the first wave of what will be a series of selections for death and were sent to the camp.

Danny does not remember whether the transport stopped short of the camp or went directly into it. He does not remember walking through the gates of Auschwitz, either (the likelihood is that he did not). What he remembers is that he was directed to the right, that his parents were directed to the left, and that as he and his group were set in

4. Refer to the appendix.

motion, he took a moment to look over his left shoulder.[5] Without comprehending what he saw, he read: *"Arbeit macht Frei."* The march to Birkenau had begun. Danny was to see his parents in a queue to the left of the tracks, along with a wash of people never to be seen or heard from again. They had boarded a truck, and it would take some time to understand what had happened. The chimney stack in plain view signified nothing special.

The process of depersonalization did not ease. For nearly two days, 320 men were locked, naked, in a small room of the sauna, and Danny, whose left forearm was now impressed with the numbers 182477, went into quarantine with Dario and the others for a period of about six weeks. This was considered the normal procedure, but it must be understood that the euphemism employed by the Germans entailed neither security nor freedom from harassment, either temporary or otherwise. He and the others were slaves, and

5. Danny remembers the following episode, which took place within sight of the boxcars almost immediately after the transport's arrival. A certain individual, noting the manner of the selection, registered that those going to the left seemed ill, older, or more frail than those going to the right. Inferring that they would get easier work to do or actual care, the man feigned a limp and winked in delight at his own cleverness. "All right," said a German. "You go over here." The man, directed to the left, now made the universal gesture of "fuck you," with flexed arm, etc., but it was he who "got screwed." In addition, Danny remembers a prisoner in the Canada work detail, later identified as Salvatore Kounio, who warned the new arrivals by whispering, "Don't say you have malaria. Don't say you have TB or typhus." While this occurred, a German took two photos of Baruch Venezia for propaganda purposes. He wished to depict the face of a typical Jewish drunkard, and he was undeterred by the fact that Baruch never drank.

they were part of a corps of men who had to perform all kinds of jobs—both meaningful and meaningless—in all kinds of weather, at any time of the day or night. Now, what this could mean is that an individual who had just returned from a ten-, twelve-, or fourteen-hour stint of forced labor could be called upon at random for another such "shift" within fifteen minutes of his arrival in the barracks. The approximately 300 men in Danny's barracks who were so affected were largely, but not exclusively, Greek Jews. Two or three similar barracks were in the same compound, but these were presumed to be made up of Jews from other countries. The men were meant to suffer disorientation, and they were meant to be broken down through a system of anarchy that rendered ego, will, and body fragile to the point of uselessness or expiration.

The prisoners were now on starvation rations,[6] but they carried guardposts at night, repaired streets destroyed by rain, removed cadavers, or transported some object from one location to another and then back again in senseless progressions of futile endeavor. The rules, if such they may be called, were stringent, for the men had to present themselves naked for certain kinds of inspection. Those who were chosen to work lived; those who were too scrawny or were ill or had come into disfavor were sent off elsewhere. Where this "elsewhere" was, Danny was to learn later. The acrid odor filled the air, and the men were hungry

---

6. The water in Auschwitz was polluted, and the men got none to drink. Tens of thousands of corpses buried in mass graves decomposed, creating an enormous upheaval in the earth. Eventually, they had to be exhumed, but by then, the underground streams had been contaminated.

and tired, but as long as they were in quarantine, none of them had the least idea of what this place was. That is to say, they knew there was a crematorium, and they fully understood its use, but there were many deaths in the camp, so that what they did not suspect was the annihilation, the genocide. A person dies. A person is cremated. This alone was understood.

◆   ◆   ◆   ◆

Danny clarifies a detail or two for me on the telephone, and I am cautiously optimistic. I tell him that I have gone on without him, and I ask whether he would like to hear what I have written. In the process, something important happens. New information breaks through, and because he is receptive, I press for exactitude.

"You went from here to here, and then what? O.K. I have it. And then what? Who was with you? O.K. I've got it. What was his name? Hmmn. Well then, what did he look like? Where was he? What kind of a smile did you say?" This is the tenor of how we proceeded, until it was understood that we would begin to meet again. "What a pity I did not meet you twenty, thirty, forty years ago," Danny says. He is not speaking romantically, and I wonder if in all those years I might have spared him a single nightmare.

VI

The Selection

Everyone knew there would be a selection. Rumors, generally reliable, filtered down from the Blockälteste and the Kapos to the men. Danny had a fever, but he wanted to present himself as being in excellent condition. He had to look healthy, and he had to be chosen. The men in the barracks felt that once they got out of quarantine, everything would be better, and Danny wanted to get out of the hellhole called quarantine. Rumor had it that the selection would be for some kind of steady job working with the dead, and that those chosen would be housed in a "fantastic place to stay." Some said that they would hear the cries of women and children when they got there, and that they would be filled with horror. This, too, was part of the "rumor mill." It shocked the men, who were being "prepared" for what was to come, but Danny prayed to be chosen.

The Blockälteste entered the barracks. He actually lived in a corner of the barracks, but he had a separate room of his own. The Kapos in Block 13 were under his direction, and it was his job to see that everything went well. "Get undressed," he said. "There will be an inspection." Three hundred men stripped; they were naked, and a German doctor entered. He was not very handsome, but he was very imposing, young and slim, and Danny was impressed. The man and the uniform seemed made of a single cloth, and the cap added just the right touch, the right polish. "It is probably Mengele," thought Danny. At the door were the doctor, the Blockälteste, and one or two Kapos.

The men, already lined the length and breadth of the barracks, now proceeded to march past the doctor. Theirs was a slow walk, and it entailed a brief stop in front of him—as he pointed to the right or to the left. He touched no one, and he said nothing. Forty to fifty men were selected. They were the youngest and the strongest, and Danny and Dario were among them—but everyone in the barracks had understood his chance of being selected on the strength of the first few choices. The men now dressed, and those selected were marched to Block 13, Lager D. The men were helpless, but the SS escorted them at gunpoint; one man wielded a machine gun. The other barracks in the compound underwent the same process. Selections were made, but none knew what lay ahead. Approximately 180 men were housed in Block 13 in all. Danny was one of fifty to have arrived, about fifty were in the block, and about eighty were out "working."

The men were shown to their new quarters, where each was to have a wooden pallet upon which to lie. They were told that they would be well fed[1]—and that the work they

1. See Marco Nahon, *Birkenau, The Camp of Death* (Tuscaloosa and London, 1989), 100–108. In this account, the initiates had abundant food and were served a few glasses of schnapps with each meal.

were to do was considered a permanent job, thereby confirming the rumors they had heard. What it was to be they did not yet know, but a French Jew struck up a conversation with Danny. They spoke in French, and the man explained the significance of not only the selections but also the smoke and smell. Danny listened carefully, but he believed he had spoken to a madman, and he laughed. He hailed Dario to his side. "Here," he said in Greek. "Listen to what this crazy man has to say." And now they all spoke in French. The ritual of initiation had begun, and it would be a long time before anyone laughed again. By the evening of the same day, fifteen of the new recruits who had been selected from Danny's barracks were to be taken on a very strange journey. Danny was among them. He was taken on a "tour" designed to shock, and he does not remember if Dario was with him at that time.

The men were marched from Block 13 to the electrically charged chain-link fence bordering Lager D. They went through this fence. Lager D was now behind them. They turned left and then left again, walked a distance, and turned right. Two structures, each bordered by an electrically charged chain-link fence, were in this compound.

"This routine continues for a few days, and each time the dosage of Schnapps is increased . . . it is distributed in greater and greater quantity. . . . On the third day, a Kapo shows up. 'Come on, lads,' he says, 'a last little glass, and then we're going to do a little work!'" The incidence of schnapps shows up in Solomon Arouq's account, too. Refer to the film *Triumph of the Spirit* (released December 1989, Orion Pictures, Los Angeles, California; Robert Young, director; Arnold Kopelson, producer). For Danny and the others, there were no such observances. They were only given an extra ration of bread at about 2:00 p.m., while they were still in Block 13.

Danny did not know it yet, but these were Crematoria I and II. They passed through one of the electrically charged fences, went down a series of steps, and entered the basement. They were now in Crematorium I, and they entered a huge room identified as the *Vestiaire*, the changing or undressing room.[2]

Danny did not know what to make out of what he saw. "My God, what is this?" This thought alone crossed his mind. What he beheld was a vast array of hooks set against the walls, heaped with clothing, and a line of benches the length of the room, overflowing with apparel of every conceivable kind. Why, half the room bulged with mounds of cloth and belts and purses, shoes, prosthetic limbs, and little bundles of all sorts. Someone said: "You can take what you want," but no one touched anything. Had the French Jew spoken the truth? Impossible! At that moment, Danny had no way of telling that 3,000 people—all of whom were Jews—had been asphyxiated.

The men were now ushered into an area no more than ten feet wide, which seemed to be a corridor of some sort. Within this corridor, and on the right, they beheld a ghastly sight Danny cannot forget to this day. "That was the turning point—the most shocking event in my life—and very important to me. It is the night I cannot recover from. I was in hell." He and the others had found themselves in front of an open, oversize door to a huge room absolutely

---

2. It was also known as the Auskleideraum. Danny uses *vestiaire*. In Auschwitz, the Sonderkommando prisoners sometimes referred to it simply as the "bunker," but on the whole they did not speak of it in any formal sense.

crammed with cadavers from wall to wall, floor to ceiling. Leaning against this door, which proved to be the entryway to the gas chamber, was an SS officer, who smoked a cigar and seemed very amused. Could he be mocking the new arrivals? Oh yes. The malevolent smile made that very clear; it was ironic and obscene, and it seemed to say, "That's what I can do to you." Danny was petrified. Never had he seen a more handsome or diabolic face, but when he heard someone say, "Clear the cadavers," he pried loose of its awful magnetism. Later on, he and the other Jews of Greece would call this man in the SS *la mula,* the mule. He was very big and strong.

Danny had no idea who had spoken, or what had become of the guardian at the gate of hell. He could not believe what he saw altogether and was utterly stupefied. What he saw *could not be,* and yet it was. It was an immovable, unshakable fact. It stayed. The dead lay there in a contorted mass, compelling him to grasp their reality. Had the soul become impervious to love and conscience? Yes. Insofar as they were concerned, it had. Within the relentless mechanism all was silent.

Danny stood in front of the door before which the SS man had derided them all, but how was he to obey the command to remove the dead? What was he to do? The tangle of bodies that lay in frozen agonies of flesh were an inabsorbable, inadmissible sight, too shattering for truth and too terrible for illusion. He had to deal with an impossible reality, but how? The fever returned, his senses reeled, and Dante's inferno came to him in a flash.

How had he set himself in motion after what he had seen? Did he know? No, he did not. Only this much is clear: he touched the first body with his bare hands, and then he collapsed. When he came to, it was to the discovery that someone had slapped him into consciousness. This kind soul was a Polish Jew—Koczak—and he took Danny aside, backtracking into the changing room and from there into a little room where minor things were incinerated. "Listen, you," he said. "You have to work, or the Germans will kill you." "But I want to work," Danny cried. In quarantine, he had acquired the rudiments of German, but Koczak would not risk a misunderstanding. He ran his finger decisively across his throat from ear to ear and warned emphatically, *"Kaput! You're gone!"*

On that day, Danny fainted four times—and each of those four times, the Polish Jew revived him at some risk to himself,[3] but it will not take long to learn this job. He will use canes to pry bodies loose and belts to drag them by the wrist to the next destination in the chain of death. Within three months, he will eat his double portion of bread while seated on a pile of cadavers. He will not be a beast, but he will not be what he was. Danny explains: "With my own eyes, I saw a German officer shoot a baby of three or four months of age once in the eye and then once in the ear, but the baby still moved its hand, so he shot it again, and then dropped it on the cement. Another time, I witnessed two SS

---

3. Koczak had some authority as a Vorarbeiter, or prisoner foreman, but it was limited. For him to have been seen by a German as he assisted Danny would have been calamitous. As it was, he extended himself very far. Danny did not work that night, and Koczak assigned him to two or three days' tasks doing routine cleanup in Block 13, allowing him to assimilate what was expected of him if he hoped to live. Danny was the only one to have fainted.

officers toss a dozen or so children in over the heads of the others already crammed into the gas chamber. Now, if that doesn't make you, let's say, different than you were before, I will be very surprised."

VII

The Process of Annihilation

Block 13 is actually the "holding place" for the Sonderkommando assigned to Crematorium II (the mirror image of Crematorium I), so that when Danny "returns to work," he reports to his "regular job." Once he is at work, he discovers there is a great deal to do and that the Sonderkommando functions as a team. The following approximates the pace and the nature of this industrialized killing apparatus.

Before the arrival of each transport, the dressing room must be cleared of every scrap of attire and every parcel. The men therefore load everything onto the trucks already in wait. Eyeglasses, shoes, etc., are piled on board, and it is assumed that all of it will make its way to Germany. It will take two hours to complete this task; however, the size of the transport dictates whether more or less time is needed. Some of the Sonderkommando prisoners will risk "organizing"[1] a gold ring here or a wristwatch there during this

1. Camp usage signifying the appropriation of goods for the purpose of survival. *Filching*. The term is derived from German usage. Refer to "The Manipulation of Language," in Henry Friedlander and

process. How dangerous this is may be deduced from the following: One day, Albert Jachon's brother and several other men in the Sonderkommando were halted by a German, while on the grounds between Crematoria I and II. The German had decided to hold an impromptu inspection. Each prisoner passed the test, but a small quantity of gold was found on Albert's brother. A little later, the witnesses to his punishment recounted that the Germans doused him with gasoline, set him afire, and instructed him to climb the wire fence, telling him that if he reached the top, they would "set him free." When he got there, however, they shot him.

It takes about ten minutes to kill 2,000 to 3,000 people in the gas chamber,[2] and the men must now direct their attention to extricating the corpses. This is quite difficult and takes about eight hours to complete. The Sonderkommando prisoners will have to hook the crook of their canes around the necks of the victims and pull very hard to untangle so sorry a human web. When this is accomplished, the body is left in the corridor; if a belt was tied around the

---

Sybil Milton, *The Holocaust: Ideology, Bureaucracy, and Genocide* (New York, 1980), 103–13. The Sephardim, or Jews of Greece, will say, "*Organizi la camisa,*" for example, "I stole the shirt." One of the men Danny knew would be able to gather a hoard of thirteen gold rings, which he would barter for a pack of cigarettes. Danny would not be a good organizer in this sense. He was interested in one thing alone, and that was whether or not a crust of bread might have survived the debacle of the boxcars. If it had, it would be ingested immediately, and it would make all the difference in the world to him. It was everything. He was not in the least interested in preserves or anything of that sort.

2. While the chambers for Crematoria I and II were below street level, access to them for the purpose of administering the lethal gas was from the roof, which happened to correspond with the street level. It was a common daily practice to see the Germans lift the protective

wrist as part of the extrication process, it is removed at this juncture. Two men, each of whom has a sack, now work on the corpses. One shaves hair, and the other removes gold teeth. Since the corridor is short and ends probably no more than five feet from this point, it is not difficult to drag the body the rest of the way to the lift, from where it is taken to the first floor. Here we find, at one end, two "dentists"[3] smelting gold and, at the other end, a small

---

concrete block, which was literally a shield approximately eighteen inches square, in order to pour the containers of Zyklon B pellets down each one of the four mesh chutes, something Danny saw done twice. The procedure was a simple one. The lid was lifted, the pellets were poured, and the lid was replaced. The pellets, activated on contact with oxygen, began the process of asphyxiation. Since Crematoria III and IV were more primitive, the method employed for murder proved to be excessively cruel. There the people were crammed into a room, and the Zyklon B was thrown in through an open window. In this manner some suffered searing burns, and all asphyxiated more slowly and torturously. The film *Triumph of the Spirit*, which deals with this theme and is filmed in Auschwitz, accurately depicts the Germans strapping on gas masks prior to releasing the lethal pellets into the chutes. Now, since Crematoria I and II had a powerful ventilating system that sucked out residues of poison gas, the men in the Sonderkommando could "safely" extricate the bodies, but Crematoria III and IV had no such "advantage." The air remained toxic, and because of the "method" employed, pellets often remained unactivated in crevices of the body. It was not unusual, therefore, for the Sonderkommando prisoners of Crematoria III and IV to have used gas masks. For one day only, at about the time of the arrival of the Hungarian transports, Danny and Marcel Nadjari were made to extricate the bodies of those so gassed. At that time, neither was given a gas mask.

3. These were not actually dentists; they were men who had been assigned to pull gold fillings and teeth from the dead and then smelt

room often used to kill small numbers of people, as well as a ladder, which leads to the second floor and the Sonderkommando cots. Between these two areas are the fifteen ovens of the crematorium.[4]

Once the gas chamber has been cleared, it must be hosed free of all traces of blood and excrement—but mainly blood—and then it must be whitewashed with a quick-drying paint. This step is crucial, and it is done each time the gas chamber is emptied, for the dying have scratched and gouged the walls in their death throes. The walls are embedded with blood and bits of flesh, and none on the next transport must suspect that he is walking into anything other than a shower. This takes two to three hours.

---

them down. As a result of their work, they could survive "on the purchases" they made out of the little they smuggled from time to time. Danny remembers seeing a German pass by the open window of the room in which the men worked. One of the dentists, who had been roasting some kind of tidbit at the time, offered a morsel to a German with a sweep of the hand. After having consumed a forkful, the two chatted amiably before the German went on.

4. Refer to the appendix. There were five installations containing three ovens each. Between three and eight persons were consumed within a given oven in a single operation; thus between 45 and 120 persons might be burned at a given time. Both the size of the transport and the size of the body affected this figure. One of the grim facts to surface was that "men are harder to burn." Since women have more body fat than men, it took less time to burn them; in addition, that body fat acted as fuel and facilitated the process. Thus, if "too many men" came up the lift at once, a backlog developed at the ovens. Now, since these must operate "efficiently," it was not uncommon for a Sonderkommando prisoner to ask for "a woman" or sometimes "a fat woman." Danny's precise words are, "It was easier for them to manage it."

The work is not yet done. The Germans and the Sonderkommando take their places in the *vestiaire,* ready in wait for the incoming transport. The Germans will patrol, and the Jews—the Sonderkommando—will assist whomever they can, for there are many old and infirm people who need help in undressing. Sometimes there will be an exchange between one Jew and another—that is to say, the victim and the Sonderkommando prisoner, who is also a victim. A sense of doom will have settled in on the new arrival, and he will submit to the Sonderkommando, whom he has assumed has a modicum of power, a document here, a photo or a letter there, to be delivered "after the war," but of course none of this is possible. And so, this is the cycle that is the order of the day. It never lets up; it only accelerates.

In two or three weeks, it no longer will be efficient for the Sonderkommando to go back and forth from Barracks 13 to the Crematoria. Hosts of Hungarian Jews arrive on the transports, and one after another, perhaps some 600,000 in all by Danny's estimate, they spill out onto the selection platform. Since most of them are slated for death, the men in the Sonderkommando are now so busy at the killing center that the Germans deem it a waste of time for them to go back and forth between Block 13 and Crematorium II. It is too inefficient, and the men are transferred to Crematorium II, where cots have been set up for them on the second level. Under this new arrangement, if Crematorium I is busier than Crematorium II, the men "will help out," and indeed, they do just that. They go from one crematorium to the other.

The Sonderkommando prisoners see themselves as "living corpses"; that is to say, they are alive, but they are consigned to death with no possibility of reprieve. Life expectancy may vary from two to three months to perhaps as long as six months, but after that, the men are eliminated. At "maturation time," therefore, the Germans shipped approximately one-fifth of the Sonderkommando work force to another camp[5]—let us say to Maidanek, for example—to be exterminated. In this manner, disruptions at the crematoria were kept to a minimum. The only departure from this "norm" known to Danny involved the execution in Auschwitz of twelve prisoners of war, all of whom were non-Jews. These men had made a futile attempt to escape and, as punishment, were placed in the Sonderkommando. In the Sonderkommando, however, they became involved in the plot to blow up the crematoria—and somehow were found out. Danny and the men who were present at the time were ordered to "go

5. In actuality, deceptions were carried out, whereby the men in the Sonderkommando of Birkenau were gassed within the camp. See Kitty Hart, *Return to Auschwitz* (New York, 1982), 125, which refers to an occurrence in the fall of 1944 and involved some 200 persons. See Martin Gilbert, *The Holocaust: A History of the Jews during the Second World War* (New York, 1985), 735, wherein September 24, 1944, is cited for the gassing of 200 Sonderkommando prisoners in Auschwitz Main Camp (possibly the same event). Also see Martin Gilbert, *Auschwitz and the Allies* (New York, 1981), 331. Some thirty persons were gassed in Crematorium IV on November 26, the very day that Heinrich Himmler ordered the shutdown of the crematoria. René Molho, an informant who was a prisoner in the main camp for something like three years, corroborates that some of the men in the Sonderkommando were put to death within the main camp. An alarm sounded the onset of Blocksperre, or a general lockup, and thus, the process was initiated while all prisoners were confined to quarters. Molho, who worked in the Canada complex at the time, had opportunities to circulate around and obtain information not readily accessible to others.

upstairs" after the Russians had been rounded up. He then heard one of the younger Russians cry out, "Koczak," but Koczak could not do anything. The shots rang out, and later on, those who worked at the ovens found the remains of the Russians' belts in among the ashes.

VIII

The Smile

By August, Europe was virtually drained of its Jewish population, and the transports arrived in erratic spurts, so that sometimes 200, and not 2,000 persons, spilled out onto the selection platform. These few Jews would not be gassed in a chamber that "accommodated" ten times as many people; at least, not for long. It was too uneconomical, too wasteful of the Zyklon B.

Crematoria I, III, and IV underwent no change and continued to operate as before, but Crematorium II was divided in two on a one-third, two-thirds basis. A well-insulated door and wall were built at the farther end of the gas chamber, and Danny and the others in the Sonderkommando were reassigned. He now had to work at pulverizing human bones, which were then shoveled onto trucks and dumped into the Vistula.[1] In this connection, Danny re-

1. Both Filip Müller, *Eyewitness Auschwitz* (New York, 1979), and Primo Levi, *Survival in Auschwitz* (London, 1959), refer to how the Greek Jews sang lustily as they worked. When I asked Danny about

counted the story of Alberto Errera (*Errera de Larissa*),[2]
Hugo Venezia, and a third person in the Sonderkommando all
of whom were asked to bring their shovels along on one
such mission. Alberto took his shovel, struck the SS guards,
and made a futile attempt to swim the river. Hugo and the
other man did nothing, out of fear. When the Germans,
who were merely stunned, "came to," Alberto was shot and
retrieved. Once in camp, however, Alberto's cranium was
sawed in half; his chest and below were hacked open, and he
was eviscerated. The corpse was laid out in this manner,
and the men were made to march past and view the body as
an object lesson. (Alberto, a Sephardic Jew who was a
former lieutenant in the Greek army, would be the bravest
person Danny got to know in the Sonderkommando, and
Hugo would be among those to be killed during the
abortive uprising at Auschwitz.)

The plan for the newly restructured Crematorium II
entailed gassing smaller groups in the farther end of the gas
chamber and larger groups in the remaining area. This was
more or less what happened, but exceptions did occur.
These exceptions had to do with the erratic pattern of the

---

this, he said he knew of no such thing, but that on occasion a
Sonderkommando prisoner might sing a song of longing while on his
cot in the loft. This was terribly painful and sorrowful; it led to tears
and was taken as a counterindication.

2. In late Autumn 1980, Polish schoolchildren planting a tree
uncovered a thermos within whose flask was a message written in
Greek by a man named Menasche, a Sephardic Jew. Along with other
data, Menasche specified that more than 300 Greek Jews were among
the men in the Sonderkommando preparing for the revolt and
mentioned Errera by name in this context (Gilbert, *Holocaust*,
743, 889–90).

transports' arrival. Thus, if the smaller chamber was occupied and another transport arrived, the larger chamber might have been used for any number of persons. As new transports arrived, however, the smaller chamber was "tended to" when there was time, but the larger chamber functioned at all times. Despite the foregoing, the system still proved its efficiency because there were fewer people to process and a smaller area to clean. After splitting the chamber in this way, and employing the technique described, it was not unusual for the smaller of the two chambers to remain sealed and intact with its complement of people for as long as four or five days or longer. When the door finally was opened, the Sonderkommando was assaulted by an overwhelming stench and the ghastly sight of putrid flesh. The bodies had turned blue and were bloated to double and treble their normal size, and Danny was among those who had to extricate them.

In isolated cases, where fifteen or so persons were brought in, the chambers were not used at all; these persons were sent up the lift, usually one at a time, and shot in front of the ovens.[3] Danny recalls two memorable instances of such shootings. One involved a Dutch Jew who had to await his turn up the lift. The man was sure to die, for he heard a shot ring out after each person who preceded him had arrived at the first level. "Well, he went absolutely crazy," says Danny. "He outstretched his arms, as if in an open embrace, and began to sing 'The Blue Danube' as he ascended. *Ta ra ra/ra-ra/ra-ra/ra-ra.* . . .'" The awful thing

3. A Sonderkommando prisoner was placed in front of the victim, who generally was shot in the back of the neck. When the victim fell, the Sonderkommando prisoner dragged the body to the nearby ovens.

that impressed Danny in all this was that the SS[4] shot the Dutchman and completed the melody without losing a beat.[5] The other instance involved another officer, also in the SS, and took quite another turn. A woman, perhaps a Viennese Jewess who had sung at the opera house in Vienna, came up the lift to be shot, but the SS recognized her. "Why, aren't you so-and-so," he asked. "Yes, I am," she replied. "Well, I've seen you perform!" What excitement. He had seen her in such-and-such a role; he loved it, and he thought she was a first-rate opera star. They chatted and reviewed the cultural life of Europe as they sat on a bench in front of the ovens, and the SS offered her a cigarette, but when their visit was over, he shot her. When this seemed rather sadistic to me, I said so to Danny, but he corrected me. "Oh no, it wasn't," he said very clearly. What had shocked me had "thrilled" him, and he went on to explain: "First of all, this German showed some sign of humanity, of having belonged to the world, which was exceptional, and second of all, this was the only man in the SS who was known to have smiled from time to time."

◆   ◆   ◆   ◆

During another interval, I asked Danny whether or not it mattered to him that Dario and he were together, and he said, "Yes," but when I asked him how this may have been expressed in daily terms—whether in Block 13 or in Cre-

4. This was SS Oberscharführer Müller or Mueller. Müller/ Mueller had a gold tooth, which Danny believes was on the right side of his mouth, but he does not remember whether it was an upper or a lower tooth. When Müller/Mueller spoke, the gold was visible.

5. Danny says of this event that it was the most terrible thing he remembers.

matorium II—he had nothing to say. "Were your bunks close?" "No." "Did you share food?" "No." "Didn't you help one another?" "Later on," he replied. Danny became pensive, and I followed suit. "There was a guy," he offered at last, "who was in Block 13—a Jew from northern Greece, a lawyer. He always said to us 'Be courageous,' but, of course, he died." That man was Markezini from Iannina.

I begin to understand the emotional drain of friendship in a place where death is so prevalent that to lose anyone else one cared for would wreak such havoc as to make absolute cruelty the mere seed of savagery, and yet, in other parts of the camp, this may have been the very inspiration for life. I also begin to remember the vignettes described by Danny. There will be Kaminsky, the Oberkapo at Crematorium II, who was known to have stomped a Sonderkommando prisoner to death and would not hesitate to kick anyone who stood in his way, but whom Danny nevertheless sees in the changing room—comforting a little girl in his lap before she is taken to be gassed. Despite the harshness and, yes, brutality of his conduct, there is something to Kaminsky, and—when given the chance—he will join in the revolt to blow up the crematoria.[6] There will be

6. Kaminsky, who was thought to be omnipotent because he was Oberkapo over all the crematoria—and was the only one who could move about freely—was nevertheless shot by Hauptscharführer Moll, once at the base of his neck and once through the left eye (Müller, *Eyewitness Auschwitz*, 152). Given Moll's penchant for sadism, Kaminsky's death was uniquely moderate; the shattering of his eye, perhaps excessive, was scarcely Moll's signature.

According to Müller, Kaminsky's death depleted the Underground of one of its best men, and threading through the tale he has to tell are unquestionably humane accounts of Kaminsky's good deeds. *Was the*

the men in the Sonderkommando who take it upon themselves to divert Hugo Venezia to Crematorium I, so that he
may not see or be a party to the putting to death of his own
father, Baruch Venezia, in Crematorium II. "Why are they
killing me," Baruch will ask of Danny and the others. "I am
still strong. I can work!"[7] And there will be Marcel Nadjari, and his mute narratives—impersonations—of the Germans, of the Jews, of the state of bewilderment in the
changing room, of entering the "showers," and in short the
entire process of extinction from the revving of German
motor bikes to the very end. Yes, even the Poles, who were
not compassionate—with the exception of Koczak—and
who ridiculed the Greek Jews for not knowing how to speak
Yiddish, wept when they saw Marcel.

There is something else I will remember. It will be the
strategy of emotional conservation, and the limits of ad-
missibility: A German officer disliked Danny and gave him
a resounding blow across the face each time he saw him.
"Pow!" Danny enacts the force of the blow and staggers
backwards, slumping to the wall. Repeated though they
were, Danny never reacted to these blows. Finally, Marcel
cried out in exasperation: "Move! You don't have to be so
philosophical!" But Danny had felt nothing; he had learned
how to desensitize himself. Today, when he looks back on
that time, he wonders if it is right to say that he had become a
Musulman. After long reflection, he decides that he had not.

---

brutality the price for the privileges bestowed upon him—the privileges that
allowed him to play a consistently strong hand in the Resistance—or did the
system produce this seemingly polarized man?

7. Danny knew both Hugo and Baruch in Salonika. According to
him, the father was not only strong but also had remained so to the
very end.

IX

The Questions

A year passes. Danny has a grandson, and I write a play. The infant is called Daniel Bennahmias.[1] And so, the name is to live; it is to move away from the dire past and sink its roots into a new land and a new life. I call my play *The Ride on the Wind*, but for some months, I do not realize that its genesis lies in one of Danny's anecdotes. Meanwhile, as much of the manuscript as has been written up to this point is hand delivered to the director of the museum at Auschwitz.

When we do meet at last it is because we are both strengthened to share what we can, but we are not in a hurry, and in fact, we do not rush. We have coffee, and we speak of music. Old concerns surface, and new questions remain unanswered. . . . Danny frets. He is uncomfortable with pessimism, but the global situation leaves little to optimism.

1. Sephardim deem it an honor to name a newborn child after the living. Ashkenazim commemorate the deceased.

So much has been written about the holocaust, and so much has been seen on television and in film, and yet, anti-Semitism is still rampant. Perhaps it is more rampant now than at any time since the war—and Danny is troubled, deeply troubled. Astonishingly, there are those among us who do not believe the holocaust happened at all. It is a hoax or a fiction, they say. Propaganda. To what avail then is it to wish or say, "Never again"? He would like to know what he or we can do to make a difference. Can we reinvest that which is civil back into *civilization*? Is there a way, a method? Can we unify words with meaning, action with intention? The answers are elusive, but Danny would like to find the key to unlock this mystery; he would like to open all the doors that constitute barriers to understanding. He is not a dreamer, but this is his dream.

He focuses on the Poles. If they do not understand their involvement, if history and facts are erasable, if memory fails, or if language must stand in isolation of the life in which it is steeped, is there any hope for mankind? What kind of men have we allowed ourselves to become, anyway? And then he remembers the people in the cities, the peasants and the partisans who slaughtered some of the Jews who had managed to escape, survive, or return home. It is a very sobering aspect of history, but he knows of no persuasion or incantation against the indifference or torrent of the storm.

He focuses on the Germans, too. "Some of us did awful things, but we say we were not free, that a gun was at our heads, that we behaved as we did out of necessity, and that this is not who we really are. We see only too readily that in our case there were extenuating circumstances, but what of the Germans who may have been similarly trapped? Is it not true that they were under compulsion to follow orders, and is there not a price to be paid for defiance to authority? Is it so easy to forfeit one's life? In brief, didn't the system create them, even as it affected us?" Disturbing as these questions may be, other equally disturbing questions arise. For example, do we not rationalize away a man's responsibility for his acts when we construe a broad chain of events that render him impotent in matters of choice? Are we mere automatons, ever subject to the sweep of the currents? When and how does culpability enter? And what would I have done, anyway? Do I really know?

I tell him that he knows, but that he does not know that he knows. I remind him that he had ample opportunity to hurt and exploit in the name of a narrow but crucial survival, but he challenges me. "How do you know I wouldn't do it?" he argues. "Because you didn't do it," I answer. "Or did you? Is there something you've kept back? Tell me now, so that we may clear this up." "Well, I didn't." "Uh-huh." "The system can do this to anyone," he says. He is very emphatic. "It didn't do it to you, and it didn't do it to your friends," I persist. "You told me you helped one another. Do you want to explain or change that?" No, he doesn't. He ponders for a while, and then he retrieves the names of the three friends from Salonika with whom he associated: Saul Hazan, Marcel Nadjari, and Leon Cohen (who has since written his own account, *From Greece to Birkenau*).[2] The "four partners" *organized* for survival. So-

___

2. Perhaps out of an instinct to mythologize, perhaps out of the depths of a colorful nature given to embellishment, or perhaps as a result of other causes, Leon would claim that Alberto Errera killed a German while dumping ashes into the Vistula, and that Hugo and the

and-so got this, so-and-so did that, so-and-so did the other.
Mostly they got food. And then they shared. Leon Cohen
and Saul Hazan were incredible at this; simply the best, but
the thought of Leon evokes a fond chuckle at the welling of
memory. "He was so good at stealing!" To this day, there is
in Danny a sense of awe at the ingenuity of this man's
enterprise. . . . "And what did you do, Danny? What did
you bring to the group," I ask. "Nothing. I was the para-
site. They took care of me. I was the youngest." He tells
me a funny story. "Once, a bag that had been organized was
placed before us to be shared. 'But this is my bag,' I cried.
That was quite a surprise." Soon I hear another story.
There was a Greek Jew in the Sonderkommando by the
name of Albert Jachon, who was either from Athens or
Salonika. This Jachon, although not one of the four partners with whom Danny participated, did what he could to
look after Danny, and once he got him some liver. The
Germans had access to beef, and every so often, a huge
quantity of rancid liver was brought to the Sonderkommando for "cremation." Now, this liver, although green or
blue with discoloration, sometimes revealed a patch that
was less badly spoiled, and when this happened, Jachon

---

other Sonderkommando prisoners were severely beaten. According to
Danny, however, this was highly improbable on several counts. First of
all, others besides Leon would have known about anything of this
magnitude; second of all, the reprisal for such a "crime" would have
been exceedingly harsh and exemplary, particularly in Crematorium II,
which was "home base" for these men; and third of all, Hugo was not
beaten. Danny would have known about this since they were friends of
long-standing who not only worked together but also saw one another
every day. (Danny did not know the third man in the Sonderkommando, who was selected at random.)

remembered his friends. This once, he remembered Danny. Naturally, had he been caught, Jachon would have had to pay dearly for his infraction. Danny's resistance melts. "I know, but I don't know that I know." Somehow, this amuses him immensely. Months later, I learn that his cousin, Jenny, had made every manner of inquiry about him—that she had persevered until she succeeded in locating him, and that she once risked severe punishment, if not her life, in order to throw a pair of socks to him from over the electrically charged wire fence.

X

The Revolt

Giuseppe (Joseph) Barouh[1] was a Greek Jew who had lived in Salonika and had served as a lieutenant in the Greek army; he was married to Baruch Venezia's daughter, Margot, and was called "Pepo" by his friends. It was from him that Danny learned not only about the plan to blow up the sauna and liberate the camp,[2] but also what was expected of him. He was informed that within a week someone would start a fire, that smoke would pour out of a window in Crematorium IV, and that this would be the signal to look out for. For the time being, and for the sake of security, however, the exact day of the rebellion had to be withheld, but it was understood that the

1. His name may appear in other accounts as Joseph Baruch.
2. Birkenau was not to be free in isolation of Auschwitz I, and the Main Camp was to work in concert with the Sonderkommando. As the Allied forces neared, however, positions wavered, and the unity necessary to free the entire camp collapsed. From this point on, the situation of the Sonderkommando prisoners deteriorated both rapidly and decisively.

signal would be given between the hours of two-thirty and three in the afternoon. Clearly, then, the action was to coincide with the changing of the guards, an event that took place at the base of the sentry posts, inasmuch as the guardhouses themselves were perched high above ground level. In the immediate vicinity of Crematorium II, therefore, the central rendezvous point involved an encounter with some thirteen or fourteen men in the SS—all of whom were trained and armed with machine guns. Now, since only one or two SS relieved the men on duty at each tower, we may assume that there were more than seven towers nearby. In addition, we may assume further that between their superior force and the advantages of their position, the Germans were well able to maintain full control over any irregularity that might erupt. So much is simple.

Stated in the barest possible terms, there were two stages to setting the revolt in motion; the first entailed gaining control over each crematorium, and the second entailed gaining control over the larger body of guards who surveyed the grounds from above. What held true for Danny and his companions not only may help to suggest the desperation of the situation but also may serve as an index to the kinds of problems the men in each of the crematoria had to face.

During the first stage—and at the designated time— two areas were to be targeted: one was the area where there were many airport guards[3] and, therefore, a commensurately larger prospect of securing a greater quantity of guns; the other was the hot water tank in the main camp. Each was to be dynamited. Within Crematorium II,

3. The airport Kommando would attack these. It was generally known that there was such a Kommando.

a Polish Jew, who was in the Sonderkommando with his brother, had to slash the tires of, or otherwise render ineffective, a bicycle, thus cutting off a minor but perhaps significant avenue of communication. Danny, Dario, and still another Polish Jew were to run from either the furnaces or the loft—one of the two places where they were likely to be—to the floor below, or ground level. There they would have to overwhelm, incapacitate, or kill the armed SS guard stationed over them within the crematorium itself. They had to do this, even if it meant that they were to use their bare hands; it was essential, because the crucial thing was to gain control over the gun. With weapon in hand, they were to run out of the crematorium and down the path that led to the manned tower between Crematoria I and II, where they were to join the others in the next stage of the assault:[4] overcoming the thirteen or fourteen armed SS, and securing the weapons that provided a modicum of hope for mastery over fate. It was of no consequence that none had used weapons or knew how to operate them.[5]

The scheme involved an absurd convergence and a vague acceptance of the notion that the many weak could have the capacity to defy the few strong. Given the circumstances, were they madmen? No. Well then, were they heroes? No. These were men who had nothing to lose.

---

4. There were no specific instructions for the "next phase" of the operation in the formal sense, because there were too many imponderables. It was generally understood, however, that if the Sonderkommando prisoners had arrived at the juncture between Crematoria I and II during the time the guards were there, they would then take part in the attempt to overwhelm the Germans.

5. Here we address ourselves to the case as it applied to Danny, Dario, and the Pole.

In the main camp, simultaneously with the action[6] at the crematoria, others were to blow up the showers, "real showers," which were used by the prisoners during select intervals. These showers were called "the sauna"[7] by the Germans—in deference to the huge tank in which water was stored—and had no special strategic value until now. If successfully executed, however, this phase of the operation could create havoc and thus provide the diversion necessary to deflect from the main thrust of all their efforts. If everything went well initially, they were not only to go on to liberate and secure the entire camp, but also to hold it for a period of two days, at which time it was presumed that Polish partisans would come to their aid from out of the woods. Given the circumstances, the rationale for the two-day lapse escapes comprehension.

The particulars of specific aspects of the plan were not known, but once apprised, one could infer simple things. Thus, if one hopes to blow up a huge installation, let us say, it does not stretch the imagination too far to suppose that dynamite may be involved. And such was indeed the case. Danny knew this as a general proposition and a logical extension of the little he had been told, and no more,[8] until the following events occurred.

6. The Sephardim used the Greek word *ntou* (pronounced "du"), which means "movement," "attack," or "revolt." It is a slang term.

7. Thousands of persons could be and were accommodated here at a given time for delousing, disinfection, and removal of body hair (Hart, *Return to Auschwitz*, 101).

8. Danny did not know that there was a munitions plant located near the railroad siding of Auschwitz I, in which the prisoners were employed as forced labor.

One day, the Oberscharführer[9] was present at the morning roll call in Crematorium I,[10] accompanied by three or four armed SS. "All right, now," he said. "Where is the dynamite?" Obviously, something had gone wrong. He pressed his hand to his side, over the pistol suspended from a belt around his waist. This was the first warning. No one moved, and no one spoke. No one dared. If someone knew something, he was of heroic stature. The Oberscharführer slid his hand across his abdomen, underscoring the implied threat,[11] but once more, there was the silence. "Get undressed," he commanded.

The men undressed in lines of five and put their clothes down on the cement floor, but Danny's things fell in an area that was wet—for the floors around the ovens had just been mopped—and he instinctively tried to place them more suitably. When he did so, however, a German signaled that he would not need them any more. This was construed as an ill omen, but another occurrence also boded ill, for Danny now lit the cigarette butt he had salvaged before relinquishing his clothes—and not one of the Germans raised an objection. "Oh-oh, that's bad news," Danny whispered to Nadjari, who was in line near him.

And now, the Sonderkommando was made to file into the

9. This was the same Oberscharführer who killed the Dutchman to the tune of "The Blue Danube," SS Oberscharführer Müller/Mueller.

10. The count is perfunctory. The attitude was that these were not men but, rather, *Stücke,* things or items. The Germans did not see the Jew as a man.

11. The ominous intent of these gestures was ludicrous inasmuch as the Sonderkommando prisoners were right above the gas chamber and in front of the ovens.

Müllbrenner, the small room where garbage was incinerated, five at a time, naked as they were. Not a sound was
heard. The men went in, but they did not come out. Danny
and Marcel put their arms around one another's shoulders.
"Well, that's it," they seemed to say, for they did not speak.
In their judgment, the men were being injected with phenol,
for they had heard that such things were being done. In
point of fact, however, they were "issued" other clothes.
"Take whatever you find," the Germans said.

Everyone knew what came next. Retaliation would be
sweet and sadistic; it would be designed to erode morale as
it weakened physical resistance, and not surprisingly, it
would be called "sports." For two grueling days of forced
labor, under conditions of starvation and armed guard, the
men carried stones, tree trunks, and timber from one place
to another, loading and unloading them senselessly. Somehow, they had managed it all without food, water, reprieve,
or loss of life—but no one knew by what formula.

Shortly thereafter, as Danny awakened from sleeping on
his pallet in the loft, Shlomo Venezia came up to him. "Let
me show you something," he said. About the distance of
two cots from where he had lain, Danny confronted two
gaping, squarish holes in the wall and knew that he was
looking at the former hiding place of the dynamite. Someone had betrayed its location, and someone else had discovered that betrayal. From the evidence before them, that
someone had had to work very fast indeed, and it was now
rumored that the cache had been stored in the area of the
vestiaire. Shlomo's news had been both good and bad. The
dynamite had been salvaged, but the holes remained to
invoke terror. None of this was a laughing matter, but some
time later, the hole was covered. Danny knows neither when

this was done nor by whom. The timing of this event was approximately two days after their completion of compulsory "sports."

At last, those involved in the rebellion were told when to expect the fateful day. Within two hours of the appointed time, however, an event occurred that brought everything to an abrupt halt. An unexpectedly tremendous number of German guards had arrived with a huge transport of Hungarian Jews and were to remain until morning. Even out of desperation, it would have been too perilous to go ahead, and under the circumstances, everyone was notified accordingly.

Now, who was responsible for masterminding the plot, detailing surveillance, establishing communication, and coordinating such maneuvers as they were capable of? Pepo? No. Pepo may have been an important link in the chain of command, but he was not the command. A high-ranking officer in the Russian army was himself a prisoner in the main camp, and it was he who was widely credited for the strategies employed in the attempt to liberate Auschwitz and Birkenau.[12]

About two weeks after the revolt had been cancelled, between the hours of two-thirty and three in the afternoon, and without prior notice to anyone, smoke was seen as it poured out of one of the windows in Crematorium IV. There it was. The prearranged signal had come from the prescribed place, in the allotted time frame, but in an unauthorized or problematic manner. Through serious miscalculation, and a colossal quirk of circumstance that was to

12. He also was felt to have been responsible for contacting the partisans.

presage doom as surely as in any Greek drama, the rebellion had been sent reeling into the throes of its abortive end. In brief, the hesitation to act was superseded by the idea that an emergency had arisen that prevented the alert from being given beforehand, and the technicality was swept aside. How could anyone have known or guessed that a "crazy Hungarian,"[13] totally unaware of the plot, had consciously set his pallet afire?

Danny and the others in Crematorium II did not see the smoke on that day and had no way of learning about its precipitous cause; they were in no position to know either one or the other. These, and other details connected with the fate of the Sonderkommando in Crematorium IV, were related to him by Isaacquino Venezia,[14] who not only was in the Sonderkommando there but also was an eyewitness to the events. Isaac, who had managed to escape through the forest separating Crematoria I and II from III and IV,[15] was able to mingle with and be absorbed by the surviving men in the Sonderkommando from Crematoria I and II largely due to his courage and the state of heightened agitation that prevailed during the next few hours, as well as in the next day or two.[16] It certainly was impossible for him

13. Danny's term.

14. Diminutive. Literally "Little Isaac," but in actuality a term of endearment. Isaac came from Salonika, had a beautiful singing voice, and was regarded as an exceptionally courageous man. He was not related to the other Venezias referred to in the account.

15. The area was quite vast.

16. Since Crematoria I and II suffered their casualties, too, the Germans combined the survivors of each and then distributed their numbers equally between the two crematoria. In this manner, each crematorium was to have the same number of "workers" with which to

or anyone else—no matter how brave—to have achieved anything like this feat at any other time. "Normal" conditions did not allow for it; the Germans were too methodical, and the control too pervasive. It therefore remains to be said that through Isaac, in stolen moments during circumspect intervals following the uprising, Danny learned of how the 400 Sonderkommando prisoners from Crematoria III and IV were made to lie naked, face down to the ground, and in rows of five, a standard German line-up procedure, before being shot and killed. As to the actual disposition of the bodies, we are led to conjecture that they were burned in the huge, open pit adjacent to Crematorium IV, since none of the Sonderkommando was assigned to cremate them.

For Danny, the element of surprise was very great; it was, in fact, a stunning blow, a highly irregular and shocking reality to absorb. There was this infinitesimal chance that things would work out, and it gave the prisoners a kind of permission to feel, to dream of perhaps being human again, but some sense of the quality of the commotion that burst in on them told the men—told Danny—that something had gone wrong within seconds of hearing the first shots and the cry of someone nearby shouting, *"It's on! We're going to move!"* In the din, and amidst sporadic gunfire, a confusing array of emotions collided with one another in rapid succession. Nothing had happened as it should have.

"keep things going." It was during this process that Isaac's opportunity arose, and the men then "closed ranks" around him. Danny, unaccustomed to the use of superlatives, refers to Isaac's achievements as nothing short of "fantastic."

Danny and ten or fifteen men in the Sonderkommando were in the loft of Crematorium II when the shooting broke out; this was their "rest period," a time to relax, the only time they had in which to restore themselves before "the next shift began." The sound of gunfire was the first indication that something momentous had happened, and then, *"Let's move!" "Out!" "The revolt's started!"* A moment of pandemonium, a moment of hesitation, and then the intermingling of fear and hope asserted itself. Everyone had been taken by surprise, but the willingness to act and the capacity to mobilize, innovate, and achieve were very great indeed. Whatever else may be said, the accidental fire in Crematorium IV was, after all, a false signal, too.[17]

Can we reconstruct where Danny was in that moment? No, we cannot. He does not remember either standing still or walking about; whether he sat at a table or lay on a cot. Pockets of memory are lost, and pockets of memory await retrieval; pockets of memory freeze into photo-stillness, and pockets of memory are thrust into the dungeons of the mind, too dangerous for freedom or parole. What has remained is a vivid picture of being just a few paces from the steps leading to the floor below, where the fifteen ovens were. He recalls going down a few of those steps, two or three at most, that he has a sense, but not the certainty, that Dario was with him, and that almost instantly he reversed himself to return to the loft in dumbfounded amazement.

17. See Müller, *Eyewitness Auschwitz,* 156, for his perception of this event. Please note that Müller's reference to "crematorium 4" corresponds to what we have consistently designated as Crematorium III. The actual date of the revolt is October 7, 1944, but Danny remembers only that it was October and not September, as alleged by other Greek survivors (see p. xxi, n. 9).

There is no recollection of the Pole, but then, he could have been anywhere in the building, "doing the work" of the Sonderkommando. What had Danny seen in that split second to have made him recoil? What had he heard?

From the window looking out on a path that served as a road, Danny saw the flight of the SS guard—the Unterscharführer whom he, Dario, and the Pole had been assigned to kill or capture.[18] The man had run out of the building, past the yard bounded by a gate, and through the gate, locking it, and had then run down the path—all the while blowing the whistle he carried as shrilly and as repeatedly as he could. The ruckus was sure to bring the Germans to the crematoria in droves, and Danny wanted to be as far away from them as possible. He and the others who shared his view were now literally backed into a corner, where they trembled and waited for the end, fully expecting to be shot. Only Koczak remained at the window, posted like a sentinel.

The troops came, and with them came the dogs. SS Hauptscharführer Moll[19] was there among them, as was the SS Unterscharführer who had fled and spread the alarm. If things had worked out differently, Danny would have killed the Unterscharführer—or at least tried. As it was now, the man was very much alive, animated as never seen before, adrenalized to tame or kill the "animals" who

18. This was a specific assignment. There were many guards.
19. In time Hauptscharführer Moll would render the ovens of the crematoria virtually obsolete. He would order the excavation of five pits behind Crematorium IV and additional pits adjacent to Bunker 5. Two of these pits would be between 120 and 150 feet long, 24 feet wide, and 6 feet deep (see Müller, *Eyewitness Auschwitz*, 125, 130; also see Hart, *Return to Auschwitz*, 120).

dared to believe they could burst their cage. But the strong, the mighty, the well armed and well fed did not venture the cage; they would not enter the building, and the Sonderkommando could not leave it. If die they must, bullets were not so bad perhaps, but the men were terrified of the dogs.

In the areas of Crematoria I and II, everything happened very quickly in the few minutes between setting off the alarm and the arrival of reinforcements, which included two truckloads of troops and ten or twelve vicious dogs. We do not know about the internal conditions within Crematorium IV, and we do not know how Crematorium III blew up. We do not know who was responsible for this, and we may never know who the heroic among the perished were. Here is what we do know: we know that the Pole rendered the bicycle useless in the fulfillment of one aspect of his assignment, and we know that the Sonderkommando from Crematorium I put the Oberkapo from Lublin into the oven alive.[20] "We heard the screams in Crematorium II. 'A-a-a-ah! A-a-a-a-ah! A-a-a-ah!'" The Oberkapo from Lublin, as he was always called, was a criminal. "He was a real criminal, a real dog. I can't imagine a human being like that. . . . Very friendly with the Germans. He was a German! Vicious man," says Danny.

Koczak stayed at the window, paralyzed by the thought that everything had gone *Kaput*, but within fifteen or twenty minutes from the retreat to the loft, the SS Unterscharführer shouted from the yard: "*Alle Antreten!* All of you,

20. Müller attributes this act to the Russian prisoners of war (*Eyewitness Auschwitz*, 159).

gather here!" Moll, the troops, and the dogs were all below. No one moved, and then the Unterscharführer barked: "Koczak, come down! Nothing will happen! Just come down!" Koczak hesitated, but the Unterscharführer became insistent. *"Koczak!"* Koczak shrugged his shoulders. "What can I do?" he asked, and then he went down, very slowly.

They talked. Koczak and the SS. For about two minutes. "Come down; don't worry. Nothing will happen to you." It was Koczak calling to them from the yard. And they went. Not out of trust, but out of a sense of finality. The collective state of mind was in a depressive condition, and they went down very slowly, hesitating all the way. Danny does not remember whether he was in the front, in the middle, or in the back. It really did not matter. Position made no difference, served no safeguard. The shooting had stopped. He remembers that.

Down in the yard, they stayed very close to the building. Koczak was there with eight to ten Germans. A truck was outside, in the street. *"Zu fünf."* It was Koczak. "Line up by fives," he said. It was the standard way, but it was not reassuring; they could have been shot at random. Koczak went in front of the men in the Sonderkommando, and the German officers took one step back. They heard the command, "Follow us," and two or three Germans took them inside. They were on street level, the level of the ovens, but they did not go to them. At the opposite end of where the "dentists" generally worked, they were directed to a small-ish room and locked in. There were eighty persons in all, for from the time the Unterscharführer had bolted the crematorium, everybody came to the loft, and nobody was left on the lower floors. They were now as crammed together as on the transports, and incarcerated as they were, that night they could hear the bombs of the Allies[21] as they fell in the distance. In this impossible situation, they hoped the bombing was to liberate the camp and found room to believe that they might live in spite of all that had happened.

Twice that day, SS Commandant Kramer[22] came to count them, and twice the count remained the same. Eighty. Something special was happening. This was the big man, the head of the entire camp, the commandant, the person one hears about but never sees. He smiled; he was relaxed and not vindictive at all. "He saw us as animals. He was counting livestock," Danny says. "But it was serious enough for him to do the counting."

The third time the door was opened, they were confronted by an SS officer from the Politische Abteilung, a

21. A few days later, they "learned" via the rumor mill that the Allies hit one of the bunkers of the SS, and that about 200 Germans were killed. Fifteen Germans were reported to have been "trained" to cremate the bodies. Presumably, the rationale was to ensure that no Jew see the "invincible" German suffer so great a loss, but in actuality, this was probably a deliberately engendered rumor to divert attention from the 200 men in the Sonderkommando who were gassed by a ruse (see Hart, *Return to Auschwitz*, 125). Clearly, rumor as a source was both a vehicle for information and an instrument of manipulation.

22. Josef Kramer was the commandant for Birkenau from May 8 to November 24, 1944, and subsequently camp commandant in Bergen-Belsen. He was arrested, tried, and executed by the British in 1945. See Danuta Czech, *Auschwitz* (Warsaw, 1978), 19, 40. Also refer to Danuta Czech, *Kalendarium: Der Ereignisse im Konzentrationslager Auschwitz-Birkenau 1939–1945* (Reinbek, 1989), 697–98.

man so brutal that he was known as the *Malach Hamavet*,[23] the Angel of Death. "Who is responsible for the maintenance of the bicycle of the Unterscharführer," he asked. A Polish Jew threaded his way out from amongst the others. "Why did you slash the tires?" No answer. The *Malach Hamavet* raised his cane and struck him on the head. Several severe strokes, and the man fell down, but the *Malach* continued to beat him as before—until the man died. Within the chamber was the poor fellow's brother, and macabre as it may seem, it was fortunate that the Angel of Death did not know it, for he would have been induced to even greater cruelty.

Once more they were locked in the room, and even though they expected to die, the beating with the cane had been too much. They had seen shooting before, and they had seen gassing before, but they had not seen this before. Premonitions of death soared. Later in the day, ten or fifteen of those who had been incarcerated were taken out. Danny was among them. They were to remove the bodies of the men in the Sonderkommando who had fallen outside of the barbed-wire encampment that bounded Crematoria I and II. In this location, between ten and fifteen persons had been killed. All had been shot. Among them was a fellow by the name of Aaron Barzelai, a Greek Jew of about forty years of age. Danny and the others brought the bodies to Crematorium I and placed them in front of the ovens, "under the supervision" of a guard. When he and the others returned to Crematorium II, the Germans gathered

23. Hebrew. Mengele and other notoriously brutal men also were known by this name.

the entire group together, and everyone was transferred to Crematorium I. Crematoria I and II became one force, and then the force was split in two. At some time during this critical period, Isaacquino Venezia found his opportunity, and the SS came for Kaminsky.

Soon after this event, the following rumor made the rounds, along with the tureens of "soup" heavily laced with bromide,[24] which entered the crematoria area from the kitchens of the main camp: somewhere in the main camp, a contingent of prisoners were engaged in packing or storing dynamite. To what purpose, no one really knew. Maybe it was to blast earth and rock preparatory to building roads; maybe it was for something or somewhere else. In any case, "the fact is" that it was there, and that a Jewish woman, also a prisoner, supervised the other prisoners and was responsible for the inventory. Over her were the SS. How close was she to the crematoria? Not close at all. Between her at the main camp and the Sonderkommando at the crematoria lay Birkenau and a host of impediments. It was she who tampered with the inventory, and it was she who made dynamite available to the leaders of the insurrection. It was she who was executed in a public hanging as a lesson to the others, and it was she who provided just such an object lesson. But it was not quite as the Germans imagined it would be. Had she been betrayed? Perhaps. None knew, and it was idle to speculate. The Germans discovered a discrepancy in the inventory, and that was that.[25]

24. It was the habitual practice of the Germans to have the soup served in this manner in order to suppress the "sexual appetites" of the prisoners. This was therefore "the usual" fare.

25. The landmarks of truth, though present, were wide of the mark. As far as is now known, what happened is that five Jewish

Someone really powerful had to be in charge of smuggling the dynamite from the main camp into the crematoria area, someone with authority to go from one camp to the other. As things unfolded, all Danny could think of was that Kaminsky was that person,[26] and he was astonished that this might be so. Until the moment when Danny saw him hold a child for a few seconds before she went into the gas chamber, Kaminsky had represented the epitome of a fearsome brutality. Now, for the sake of that moment, Danny found that he could like him a little, but he was utterly amazed that someone like Kaminsky, so outwardly a part of the suppression, should have joined the rebellion.

The uprising that had begun so inauspiciously proved to be costly in the loss of life by ordinary standards, but not in

---

women were arrested by the SS in the Union armament factory nearby. These women were horribly tortured, but none betrayed either persons or plans. Four of the five were executed in a public hanging after the revolt, with all of the women at Auschwitz assembled as witnesses. Danny had heard about "the Union" from time to time, but what it was neither he nor the others really knew, as can be seen readily from the nature of what had been gleaned (see Gilbert, *Holocaust,* 743–44). Danny says, "There weren't two events." We would have to stress at this point the difficulties to be encountered in any communicative process between the men and women, inasmuch as each was inaccessible to the other and virtually in separate camps.

26. It would take years before Danny was to learn that Kaminsky could not have been the one to have achieved this feat in its entirety. Kaminsky did not have the authority to go beyond Birkenau, and the main camp was well beyond that. Thus someone would have had to bring it from Auschwitz I to Birkenau, where he could then bring it from there to the crematoria. Dr. Kulka, a scholar who resides in Israel and with whom Danny spoke in Oakland, California, has as yet not published his findings in this matter.

terms of the scale of the factories of death. Its remarkable achievement is that, from this time on, the abhorred crematoria of Auschwitz never will be used again, although both the gassings and the burning at the pits continue—and by the end of October, some 33,000 Jews or more will have been killed.[27]

Within days of the abortive revolt, Danny and the other survivors of the debacle will be set to dismantling the crematoria, brick by brick. For this purpose, a corps of slave laborers from the main camp will join them—and for the first time, among them will be women. Pola Uziel, from Salonika,[28] whom Danny knew there, will be someone with whom he can talk, and each will take heart from this. They will share their innermost thoughts, and they will speak of their past experiences with one another, even as others will be doing the same.

At about this time, Jenny, who worked near the crematoria, yearned for the sight of Danny and sought him out at every opportunity. Amazingly, this enterprisingly tenacious girl found him and succeeded in establishing eye contact, but of course neither could converse. Perhaps a word or two escaped their lips; yes, that was possible, but for the most part, the entirety of their exchange rested on a furtive glance of recognition. For a while prior to the dismantling of the crematoria she ceased to come altogether, and then suddenly, one night at dusk, she was right there at the gate. Two persons, one on either side, held her

---

27. See Gilbert, *Auschwitz and the Allies*, 326.

28. Pola, now married to a doctor by the name of Kendros, lives in Baltimore, Maryland. Her sister, Ninette, also was a slave laborer assigned to this detail.

upright. The inspiration for her visits in this saddened state had come from the rumor that had reached her; namely, that the Sonderkommando was about to leave. And so, this is how Jenny appeared during and after the dismantling of the camp. She had become a semblance of herself, an apparition, a Musulman, at the age of sixteen. Her former beauty would return, to be sure, but for now what remained was the distillation of that beauty as manifest in her spirit.

Himmler ordered the crematoria at Auschwitz destroyed on November 26; on that same day, Crematorium II had its motor crated for dispatch to Mauthausen and its conduits sent to Gross Rosen, which was, along with Ebensee, a satellite of Mauthausen, and thirty Sonderkommando prisoners were killed.

XI

The Death March

O the 16th and 17th of January, the men in the Sonderkommando were in Block 13, the isolated compound in Birkenau. They were closed off from the general camp, locked behind a wooden gate, and subjected to barracks detail. Nevertheless, one of the Sonderkommando prisoners, who had a friend in the Politische Abteilung, received a message that the Germans planned to kill them, that fifteen men had been selected to learn and do the job, and that the Politische Abteilung kept a record of the fifteen who were going to do this. The men, although concerned, were not surprised.

By January 18, the front had moved closer; the artillery fire was pronounced, and the men could now see the bursts of sporadic explosions. One sensed danger, but none more than death, and death is death. As members of the Sonderkommando, they had been fated to die from the very beginning. The thought of liberation was remote, if existent at all.

In the morning of the same day, the entire camp had

an Appell, as usual. The men in Block 13 were out of doors
for this purpose; they looked out on a team of Germans
reviewing the Appell, and when it was over, they took
note of an SS officer who called off fifteen numbers—but
nobody responded, and nobody showed up. Within seconds—
for there was scarcely time to react to the significance of
the missing fifteen—a German arrived on motorcycle with
an urgent dispatch for a high-ranking officer, and something exceptional happened. Pandemonium broke loose.
"Everybody, take your things! We are going to leave! *Alle
Antreten!*" Excitement filled the air. Needlessly, Danny
explained: "This was a big day for us."

When the gates were flung open, the men in the Sonderkommando knew that their only chance was to disperse
among the prisoners at large. From now on they neither
would talk to one another nor seek one another out; if they
chanced to meet, they would manage everything with a
look, an intensity in the language of the eyes. They had
conspired to live without uttering a word, and they would
acknowledge one another in silence. As for the fifteen men
who were to have put the Sonderkommando to death and
did not respond to the roll call, Danny surmises that in the
general confusion of the last few days in which the transports had been intensified,[1] the men had seen and seized the
opportunity to feed into one of them. The tight reins with
which the Germans controlled the camp had begun to
slacken, and it did not take much intelligence for the

1. The transports were always busy. Prisoners were often transferred to other labor details in other concentration camps throughout
the existence of Auschwitz. This, however, was different. It marked
the beginning of the death march and the attempt to empty Auschwitz
of its human cargo.

prisoners to infer that if they killed the remaining Sonderkommando, the Germans would kill them. In any case, everything was "upside down" now, and the Germans wanted to leave, too.

January 18 was a very hopeful day, "the day I remember—a day of celebration," says Danny. "Nothing mattered except to get out. To get out of the gate and to get mixed up with the others." It was the dead of winter, and they had no warm clothing, but at the risk of punishment or death they stuffed their shirts with the paper they had "organized" and took their chances. "We were extremely lucky." Danny was elated. The forbidden paper had come from the sacks of cement they had had to work with as slave laborers, and he had been able to get hold of a pair of relatively new boots. There was no way for him to guess at the tribulations awaiting them.

The first phase of the death march, from Birkenau (Auschwitz II) to Monowitz-Buna (Auschwitz III), involved an eight-kilometer walk. Some 1,500 or more persons would freeze to death, die of exhaustion or other causes, or be shot to death for the crime of lagging, but Danny continued to be euphoric. He concentrated on neither frost nor fatigue, even if he felt both. Everything was dismissed. He was no longer in Auschwitz-Birkenau. This, and this alone, was foremost in his mind. On arrival, his sense of Buna was that it may have been a camp that operated some kind of rubber industry, but that it now functioned otherwise.[2] He had come to a place of height-

2. Danny's sense of the place is essentially correct. A synthetic oil plant functioned there at a greatly reduced rate of production as a result of the bombings of the U.S. Army Air Corps (2,000 tons per

ened activity, a center of sorts, into which thousands of prisoners fed and from which they exited. Apart from these impressions, he remembers a rather large hall in which some of the prisoners stayed—he among them—and that the Germans distributed an extra ration of bread.

On the morning of the next day there was no Appell, and the prisoners were gathered by fives to begin the march. They walked in the bitter cold by day and by night. Those who fell were shot; the others were numb and nearly senseless. For four or five days this went on, and Danny's boots became abrasive. They were all wrong for such a march, all wrong for such legs as he now had. Nothing was left of the elation; it had vanished with all thought of hope. They passed a German village, and old women villified them. "*Schweinhund*," they cried out. "Take gasoline and light a match, burn them, set them afire!" Old women, without shame. Snow fell. They moved on and left the jeers behind them.

At last, they came to a big farm and poured into a barn.[3] They were so worn out that they could not lie down, and some fell asleep while seated. A nasty swelling made Danny's

---

month output down to 500 tons per month). The synthetic rubber plant, due to open on the very day of an air raid, did not open; it was put out of commission, and the Germans targeted February 1 for the completion of repairs and the opening of the plant. On January 18, however, the camp was vacated of all but the sick. For a full account of events at Buna, see Primo Levi, *Survival in Auschwitz* (London, 1959).

3. Forty years earlier, Dario had mentioned an incident to me involving a barn and how those who entered lived through the night, while those who could not froze to death. In some cases fingers and noses snapped off on contact, like so many icicles. Danny does not recall any such incident, but he feels this may have been the same barn.

feet unrecognizable appendages. Above the blue, an ugly wound bode ill, and it would be heard from again. For now, Danny suppressed all pain. On went the boots. He would need them in the morning. He functioned entirely on instinct. These were not consciously ordered thoughts. He slept as he was, discounting the purple rage and the ugly inflammation.

They walked for another half-day or so. Everyone tried to help one another whenever it was easy. They were afraid. "Come on, move; move, or they will shoot you," they said. It was still snowing when they came to a railroad station, a train stop. They had come to a place where they had to board the open wagons of an open train, and they were crushed into place as the snow covered their misery.

Danny and the others were on the train for four or five days, and maybe even a full week; the calculation was difficult under these conditions. They did not get off at all, and there was only one rather lengthy stop at Brno, which turned out to be memorable. The Czechs had lined the length of the train—men and women alike—and had thrown food to them. Bread and salami mostly. A little cheese. And suddenly, a man came into focus, a man Danny would never forget. He wore a fedora and a warm great coat with a fur-lined collar, and his bearing was of the classic sort—the sort out of which the prime ministers of England were made. He had come there with an entire wheelbarrow filled with food, which he tossed to them in total disregard of the Germans. The other men and women were heedless, too. They did not flinch; they did not stop, not even when the Germans shot into the air to dissuade them. In this manner, and because of them, Danny got a piece of bread.

At last, they stopped.[4] It was early evening, and they were near Mauthausen, which they could not see because they were on a hill. They walked a short distance, and on his right, Danny saw a woman who had frozen to death; she had been set into the ground and propped with an outstretched arm pointing directly ahead, to the camp. The Germans had used her as a signpost. "She was old; my God, she was old and wrinkled." Danny's fingers drew imaginary lines across his face; he sucked in his breath. "She was so lined!" But how could she have been old? After a while, they reached a plateau from which they could view the camp. It was huge and very well lighted.

The Germans were waiting for them; they were ready to welcome them in as they entered. Their truncheons fell upon them; blow upon blow, they descended in anarchic, impartial, blind brutality. The prisoners scattered; they ran. Even in their extremity, they ran to evade the newest ferocity to have befallen them. "*Schnell, schnell*," urged the Germans. They had a persuasive argument. "*Schnell!*" Hurry to your doom. Hurry to your death. Hurry to torment before the final release.[5]

The first night in Mauthausen prolonged their ordeal, for the prisoners slept out of doors. Danny and two others lay on the frosted ground, along what seemed to have been the corner of a building. They could have died—all were

4. The journey had taken them across Poland, Germany, and parts of Czechoslovakia (which had been annexed and divided into three regions by the Germans: Sudetenland, Protectorate, and Slovakia) before they arrived at their destination in Austria (Ostmark).

5. During the eruptions of the last two weeks or so, Danny had lost track of Marcel Nadjari and Dario Gabbai. He would meet Dario in Ebensee and Marcel after the war.

meant to die sooner or later—but Danny's body had grown accustomed to its martyrdom and was not yet ready to surrender its essence.

In the morning, Danny and the others were awakened. They were covered in frost. There was no food, no bread, no water, and no pretense of any. When they were led into a barracks, they were shuttled from one place to another. And when they were subjected to a physical examination, they were utterly naked,[6] and had been made to stream in, one at a time. But this was not a true examination at all; on the contrary, it was a determination of "damaged goods" to be discarded, and it consisted of a German doctor with an inked marker. A swift assessment and a cross drawn across the chest consigned a human being to the incinerator—like trash. It was here, during this process, that Danny learned from a fellow prisoner that 180 men who were formerly in the Sonderkommando from Auschwitz had been gassed at Mauthausen. Naturally, he confided nothing about himself.

Those who survived the doctor's selection were slated for a shower, and they were channeled to such a place indoors. They could not be sure, but they felt that these were real showers, and they were not unduly alarmed. Naked and wet, they were made to run out of doors for a distance of about two blocks in order to "get dressed." It was to take a long, long time, however, before they were given anything to wear. They huddled together in a room of the barracks as others streamed in and still others would later stream out. The group was actually in a state of flux after a while, but for as long as it was possible, they packed in as closely as they could. They sought the body heat that eluded them,

6. At this juncture, Danny lost his boots.

but the trembling did not end. It was ceaseless. It was unrelenting. It was late January, and it was freezing. Finally, they got nightshirts, which were distributed in another room. They had no pants and no underwear.[7] They were essentially naked.

Attired in shirts scarcely to be credited as articles of useful clothing, the prisoners were led into a huge room, which was totally bare. There they sat; they did not lie down, for they could not. They were too congested for anything of the sort. Once again, the density was like that of the boxcars, and once more, relieving oneself placed one at risk. There was a body or an arm, a leg, a head, an obstacle to confront and a course to complete that had to be negotiated; it required diligence. A single misstep could cost one one's life, but should any mishap occur, staying in place presented obvious danger, too. And so, this was Danny's lot; this was his block; this was his abode for four days. All in all, there were four, five, or more such blocks, each exactly alike in misfortune.

The cold held sway. There was no recollection of food. Perhaps there was a vile brew; perhaps there were a few crumbs. It is hard to say. The physical aspect was so heartless, one could not remember anything but the worst, and the worst was the Appell. "It was horrible, horrible. A tremendous sufferance. I will never forget that." Danny's tones are measured. "We were there to be killed. We were temporary." The Appells were meant to see to that.

From time to time, when the prisoners were in the bare room, the Kapos or the Germans dropped in on them; they checked up on the goods—the *Stücke,* the "things" in their

7. Danny received a pair of battered shoes selected at random.

charge, but they did not say anything of consequence. So, that was not very bad. No one paid attention. The men were not out in the cold, and that was the key. It was a relief to be in the room. Due to the inclement weather, it had, in fact, become a haven of sorts. At the Appell, however, everything said or unsaid wielded its full measure of woe, for the Appells were nothing less than opportunities for beatings and invitations to demoralization and death. This was what it meant to remain standing for hours, three, four, five, or more, perhaps—until the Germans were gratified. Exposed and miserable, some passed out and others died. Those who stayed on their feet did their best to hold on to those who fell—both the living and the dead—for what they had to do at all costs was remain in formation, *zu fünf*, by fives, if they were to avert a protraction of their agony.

And so this was their life for four days.[8] Back and forth they went from the bare room to the piercing cold, from the piercing cold to the bare room, etc. Danny's legs were now twice their normal size, and the idea of going to the infirmary did not appeal to him at all—so that was that, with one exception. They were about to move on, and it seemed to him that he must contend with another march. The Germans had distributed trousers and prison garb for them to wear, and they were on their way to Ebensee. As distance goes, it was not far. The trip took hours instead of days. This time, however, a convoy of trucks transported them to new tribulations.

8. As things were, they could have fared much worse. The commandant of Mauthausen, Franz Ziereis, was known for his cruelty. It was once his boast that he gave his son fifty Jews "for target practice" as a birthday present. See Martin Gilbert, *Atlas of the Holocaust* (Jerusalem, 1982), 233.

Danny marched in on a sorry pair of legs; he was exhausted, and yet his spirits lifted. Even in his distress, he could see that Ebensee was beautiful. He was in a forest bounded by mountains and, as he soon would learn, a region of spectacular sunsets. Snow-laden leaves beckoned; they creaked with their weight and seemed veritable marvels. He took refuge in them fleetingly, even as his eye caught the descent of the sun, but the cold was barely tolerable, and his oppression was very great indeed.

Danny's legs had taken on a life of their own. They were pus-filled, aching containers, tubular pestilences swarming with colonies of microorganisms, and he had to work twelve- to fourteen-hour-long shifts of rigorous slave labor. As a matter of form, construed idleness, or the pure sport of it, the truncheons awaited everyone. The Kapos and the Germans knew how to administer their authority; they knew how to extort the last vestige of strength, the last breath from the underling and captive. When he was in the Sonderkommando, the psychological toll of what Danny had been made to do by far exceeded any physical outlay of energy. There was no way that he could insulate himself—and he had not become inured—but there was always some way to obtain food, some way to manage a little something to offset starvation. In among the forlorn parcels that remained after the gassings, one might find a sustaining crumb to be gulped surreptitiously, a chunk of bread to hoard or share. Not so here. Here the physical dominated; here the actual was starvation. Here there was no recourse.

Men dotted an entire mountainside and strained at their loads; they scrambled in among tunnels and excavations so vast as to defy description, and they carried enormously heavy railroad ties often too large for four men to lift. The Germans envisioned yet another railroad line at this late date, and this was a very serious enterprise, a massive undertaking involving thousands upon thousands of slave laborers. A staff of engineers and a Meister for each group of slave laborers guided the operations; they exerted great power and had control over anyone with the exception of the SS—and no wonder, for the Germans' plan entailed housing twelve armament factories in these tunnels, along with all of the prisoners and in fact the entire camp.[9] The work was unbelievably hard, unconscionable.

Ebensee was the most difficult of all to bear. The snow was three to four feet high, the cold was fierce, Danny was starved, and servitude was at its highest turn of the screw. Nearing the end, and with what little remained of endurance, Danny withdrew to safeguard the last spark; he entrenched himself to conserve that which was by now barely conservable. He was more dead than alive, and he soon would move very little and very slowly—or not at all—for fear that the slightest motion, the slightest turn of the head, would snuff out that amazingly hardy and stubborn last spark.

There were a few kind people—some of whom were incidentally so. The Meister, who had ordered Danny to the infirmary in the first instance, had been "kind,"[10] and the secretary of the block, the Schreiber, a Jew from

9. See Konnilyn G. Feig, *Hitler's Death Camps: The Sanity of Madness* (New York, 1970), 126. For a detailed account of Ebensee, refer to Robert H. Abzug, *Inside the Vicious Heart* (New York, 1985), or Florian Freund, *Concentration Camp Ebensee* (Vienna, 1990) and *Das Konzentrationslager Ebensee und Die Raketenrüstung* (Vienna, 1989).

10. The Meister, noting the condition of Danny's legs, ordered him to the infirmary. This act was not literally a kindness; he was bound by the rules to do precisely what he did, but at this juncture, it served as a kindness to Danny.

Belgium who had allotted him extra days in the infirmary at some risk to himself, had been kind. Still, how long could he go on? Ill or not, for two months he slaved on dishwater and crusts of bread, and then, for an entire month, only the dishwater remained. Once, Danny found a coal-like substance, hard as brittle bone but chewable, at the base of a tree. Its taste was "nice and oily," and it was not uncommon for the prisoners to forage for some whenever they could. Once, someone found what they took to be a dog bone—it certainly was not human—and eight of them shared that. This was the level of existence, the extent of what it could be like when things were "good."

Between infirmary bouts, months of servitude and starvation, and the barbaric passive cruelty of the Appells— one of which lasted for more than eight hours because a "number," not a man, never a man, was unaccounted for[11]—well, what was this, if not the coldest hell imaginable? Danny's body was ravaged—savaged by systemic poisons—and even then, the SS sought him and others like him for particular extermination.

One night the Germans came to the barracks while Danny and one of the French Jews, a doctor attached to the Sonderkommando,[12] were lying on the same cot. It was

11. Since individuals were lined up by fives, the procedure was quite simple. Twenty lines of five persons rendered a complement of one hundred. It was a determination that could be made in large part visually. Thus, this aspect of the Appell went rather quickly. When the visual did not render the conformity expected, then the search began. The numbers of those present were taken and checked against those who were not there.

12. This was a Dr. Bendel, a man of seemingly average intellect who had no special gift for medicine but who nevertheless managed to

midnight or so. "Who here was a Sonderkommando in Auschwitz-Birkenau," they asked through an interpreter, and the French Jew began to tremble violently. Danny steadied him; he gripped his leg and held on to it as firmly as he could, for to be detected by this means spelled certain death. In brief, this happened not once, but rather many times, and inasmuch as the Germans were determined to ferret out anyone who had been in the Sonderkommando, the sense of unease increased unabated by thoughts of liberation.

Not long thereafter, it was rumored that Hauptscharführer Moll had received the numbers of the Sonderkommando prisoners from the Politische Abteilung, and that he was expressly in charge of eliminating all survivors. They were certainly sought after, and this seemed plausible enough, but whether or not it was true, Danny cannot say. At some point, Moll was captured. His trial was held in Dachau, and he was executed on May 28, 1946.[13] Oberscharführer Muhsfeld, whose death Moll accused Kaminsky of plotting moments before Moll shot him,[14] was brought to trial, too,

---

keep a supply of drugs on hand for use in the block. These mostly consisted of aspirin, which he undoubtedly confiscated from Canada, the sorting station that dealt with the clothing and parcels that remained from those who had been gassed. Dr. Nyiszli and another Hungarian Jewish doctor attached to Crematorium I were of an entirely different order as scientists, but all were eminently decent persons. Müller cites Bendel's role in aiding the Resistance (*Eyewitness Auschwitz*, 148).

13. Refer to "Extermination," in Franciszek Piper, *Auschwitz* (Warsaw, 1978).

14. Müller, *Eyewitness Auschwitz*, 152.

and he was executed on December 22, 1947, in Cracow.[15]

The sadism of these two—one of whom, Moll, was a master—was finally at an end. Never more would Moll's terrible jokes prevail. *"Say, have you a keen sense of smell? Do you smell this rose?"* These are the questions he asked before firing his gun into a victim's nostril.[16] One day, as it so happened, Danny saw Moll riding through the camp on his motorcycle. At the electrified fence within view, a Sonderkommando prisoner was "organizing" with either another prisoner or a civilian—something that was strictly *verboten,* and Moll easily and simply unholstered his pistol, aimed, fired, and shot the Sonderkommando in the shoulder without once altering either his course or pace. About two hours later, on Moll's return to camp, his first inquiry was: "Where is the prisoner whose shoulder I wounded?" His plaything only now would be ripe for other games.

15. Piper, *Auschwitz.*
16. Nahon, *Birkenau, The Camp of Death,* 107.

XII

The Reunion

We are not quite through with Ebensee, and it now remains for us to retrace our steps briefly. Let us therefore return to the first days in camp, wherein the bitter cold, the inadequacy of attire, and the insufficiency of caloric intake do the work of weaning Danny away from his fear of the infirmary.

Danny tries to haul the railroad ties as directed. With all his strength and what remains of desire, he heaves at the load, trying to make it comply with his will. Never, never, never must a Kapo or a Meister or the SS learn the secret of that fine pair of legs he keeps hidden from view with those flimsy trousers of his. The legs are hateful, absolutely horrible. He would like to tear them apart, but he does not dare. How they teem with life! He is decimated, but they thrive. The situation is desperate. Yes, he must be careful. He must not stumble. The overseers are everywhere.

What makes a man go on? He does not know. But he tries. He tries, and he fails. He is finished. The load slips; he cannot carry his end, though he tries. The wretched leg is exposed to view; the tattered trousers have betrayed him. The secret is out. It is exposed, and what is more, the overseer has seen it. The offending leg will be his death. "Go to the infirmary," says the Meister, but Danny does not want to do any such thing. He hesitates. He is a dead man whether or not he obeys.

At the infirmary, they gouge his legs. He has no anesthesia, and they have no implements worthy of the name. Who knows if they are even doctors? And who cares? Primitive or not, painful or not, he has been lanced. Venom spews out. It vomits its hostile horde and splashes onto the floor, and for the first time in weeks, he feels relief. He knows peace. Hygiene be damned. This feels good. There are no selections here. He will either live or die; there is no need for anyone to do anything more to him. Death is virtually guaranteed. The warranty is all about him. Danny has a few days of respite. He is out of the cold, and he does not labor. He does not eat, either—but then, that would have been the case in any event. There was very little to eat altogether for the first sixty days, but during the last thirty days, they get only a bit of colored water. "Well, they call it soup." Danny graciously dignifies the slop.

Between the first and second and the second and third times he will be in the infirmary, Danny will be awakened at four-thirty in the morning; he will wash out of doors, report to the Appell, and continue in laborious servitude. During his third stay, he will be liberated by General Patton's forces. In the course of one of those stays, he will meet a man who tormented both himself and Danny with fantasies about how his mother fed him entire meals made of chocolate, but his own fantasy—a modest dream—will have him drinking from an enormous goblet none other

than a hot, steaming broth made entirely of butter. The first
stay entailed "surgery"; the second, "treating" the wounds
that had burst; and the third, "cleaning out" infected
areas—without benefit of medicine, of course. There will
be no bandages, either, but paper will be used as if it, too,
can serve the same function. At this last stage of despair,
Danny loses a significant amount of weight and strength.
He is also very nearly a Musulman.

The infirmary's "design" has an order to it, and that
order is directly proportional to one's proximity to death.
Thus, the first, second, and third sections of the infirmary
are "reserved" for the least serious cases; the fourth is for
the most serious; and the fifth is for the dead and dying.
Each section is housed in a separate room. Danny's third
visit finds him in that fifth section,[1] which bears description.
Let us imagine entering it.

We look down a long corridor on either side of which we
find a series of bunks, each of which is occupied by up to
four persons. Underneath the window on the wall at the far
end and to the right is a huge pile of human beings. This
heap is made up of the dead and the dying. Sometimes it
can be seen to stir, and sometimes a faint sound may
emanate from it, but on the whole, we may say that it is still.
It is conceivable that some suffocate as others weight them
down and block access to oxygen, but it is certain that all
have been trashed. Opposite the entry is the only other
window in the room.

One day, as Danny lies on a cot, he will see a Sonderkommando prisoner from Auschwitz-Birkenau who stoked
the furnaces as a Heizer, a Pole by the name of Alter,

1. The first two stays were in the third room.

brought down the corridor assisted by an individual on either side. This man Alter, once so tall and strong, once so seemingly invincible, is tossed by the two—as a matchstick—onto the pile. The system has consumed him utterly, and all that is recognizable is the man's face. Yes. This is room five, and this is what you might have seen at any time. Another day, Pepo is brought in. Pepo. Imagine that. He not only is brought in with the aid of another, but also is placed in the same cot with Danny. Make no mistake about it. He is dying, and Danny is dying. This is what they have in common here, but a strange thing happens. A kind of rite takes place that will be among Pepo's last. Now in the advanced stages of tuberculosis—galloping TB, they called it—Pepo wants proof that he will not die, and what better proof can there be than to offer the once-only-in-a-day-slosh to Danny? If Danny eats from his bowl and with his spoon, surely then, he is not contagious, and if that is true, he could not have tuberculosis and he cannot die from it. If Danny refuses, well then, that will be a bad sign. A serious indication. And so, he drinks half and he proffers half, imploring Danny to take it "with my spoon." Danny does not refuse; he cannot, because he is starved. He takes what is offered without a shred of remorse. He has feeling, but he cannot react.[2] He can eat, but he cannot speak. He cannot get into conversation. He cannot explain. Pepo's eyes burn. They lie in sunken pits, rimmed by the aura of death.[3]

Against these motifs, still another plays itself out. The

2. We are confined to a narrow, subtle range of response, or so it would seem. (At this point, Danny thought of himself as a Musulman.)

3. Pepo died in the same cot Danny lay in within a few hours of Patton's arrival. There were four persons on this one cot. Albert Jachon also died on the day of liberation, but he was not at Ebensee.

Blockälteste, an Austrian, will rampage through the infirmary, beating the sick with his truncheon. It is not unusual; do not be misled into thinking he is alone in this, that he is perhaps more brutal than another. He is not. "Be careful! The Americans are coming! I'll kill you all!" The man is wild. One cannot run. One is simply an easy prey.

Now, this Blockälteste flees, as do many of the SS guards who are replaced by Volksdeutsche, and an extraordinary event takes place. All 30,000 prisoners who are not already dying are ordered into a tunnel packed with explosives—and the prisoners, who do not want to be blown up or gunned down, refuse to enter. They know of the approaching Americans, even as do the SS and the Volksdeutsche, and they see in their resistance the possibility of surviving the war. The SS guards, thrown into a state of indecision by a swaying, murmuring mass and a series of predictable considerations related to self-interest, hesitate. And in this fateful moment, the commandant, observing the shift, gathers some of his subordinates together for a hasty consultation. Despite their past, all concur. The war is nearly over, and they do not wish to court the punishment for so vast a slaughter.[4] For the time being, the prisoners come to no further harm, and needless to say, the Germans now flee in earnest. All but a handful are gone before the Americans arrive.

Ebensee is among the last of the camps to be liberated.[5] The Americans photograph both the abysmal plight of the prisoners and the deplorable conditions throughout. Part of

4. See Gilbert, *Atlas of the Holocaust*, 235. To my surprise, Danny knew nothing of this incident until I informed him of it.

5. Ibid., 234. Ebensee and Günskirchen were satellites of Mauthausen, even as Birkenau and Monowitz were satellites of Auschwitz. Mauthausen was liberated on May 4, Günskirchen on May 5, and

the pictorial documentation will include the infirmary, and several times in the course of each day for the next two days, Danny will see one or more persons stand in the doorway, snapping away with camera in hand. But, of course, the Americans do more than observe and record. They bring about an immediate improvement in the quality and quantity of food and set bulldozers to clearing a vast area of the forest.[6] There they will establish a sort of tent city for the sick. Food, medicine, doctors and nurses, care and compassion are now what Danny and the others experience. Unfortunately, however, a severe lesson will be learned here, for the improved diet causes a radical case of diarrhea,[7] from which an estimated 10,000 persons will die.[8] Danny's appetite suffers a temporary arrest. He, too, has diarrhea.[9] The Americans cut back the nutritional value so

---

Ebensee on May 6. At ten to three in the afternoon, the much longed-for liberation of the camp by the Third Cavalry F Company took place under the command of Capt. Timothy C. Brennan of South Belmar, New Jersey. The tanks of Sgt. Robert Persinger of Rockford, Illinois, and Sgt. Acton ("Dick") Pomante of Sterling Heights, Michigan, actually opened the camp. Two days later, on May 8, the Germans surrendered unconditionally to the Allies.

6. This was under way after the second day of the Americans' arrival. "We heard a fantastic roar for four hours." In the afternoon, the bulldozers were finished, and in the morning, Danny was in a tent.

7. Tragically enough, the British learned this a bit earlier, after they liberated Belsen on April 15. The "rich" food from the British army rations included dried milk powder, oatmeal, sugar, salt, and tinned meat (see Gilbert, *Atlas of the Holocaust*, 226).

8. As projected by Danny.

9. Danny's diarrhea was unrelated to the improved nutrition: he was in the throes of death, so to speak. What was happening to him was part of a familiar pattern in the camps.

that it is little better than what the prisoners had been accustomed to, and then, by degrees, they increase its wholesomeness. . . .

In the bunk to Danny's right is a fellow from Copenhagen, a Danish Jew who worked at the Royal Library as a free man, to whom it is inconceivable that liberation has come. "This is a trick," he cries. "Don't eat anything!" And he does not eat for quite a while, so certain is he that this is part of German deceit. Another fellow who has lost his mind sits upon a rock outside of the infirmary. Day and night, he juxtaposes the fingers of his right hand in succession, so as to form a V—a V for victory. Still another fellow, a Hungarian Jew, goes from cot to cot. "What do you need," he asks each one in turn. "What do you need? I will get it for you. I will do it." Over and again, he recites his litany, but, of course, he cannot do anything. He, too, has lost his mind. He is in dire need himself.

Elsewhere in camp, a few of the Russian prisoners take hold of the five or six Germans to have remained at Ebensee and make them clean latrines or do other menial work. The Americans object, however. "This is no way to behave," they say, and then they place the former prisoners in detention for a period of twenty-four hours. The ironic has been dealt a hand. These are not the streets of Paris surging with jubilation and righteous indignation.

Danny remains in the infirmary. He tries to walk by stabilizing himself along the row of bunks until he reaches the window. There he rests and diverts himself before retracing his steps—but on the day after liberation, something special happens. A figure pauses by the window and comes to a halt. "My God, Danny, is it you?" This is what he hears from Dario, who has fared better than he and has set out to find him. Yes. Dario and others who can do so have been on the move, looking for survivors, from the time their camps had been liberated.

Dario finds the block in which most of the Greek Jews are housed and bunks with him. He stays for something like three weeks and makes frequent visits to town for a little meat or a few choice foods with which to strengthen Danny. When a huge hospital tent is set up for the most seriously ill, this is no longer a compelling necessity. Danny is brought miniscule things to eat and is ministered to every ten minutes or so. He has a cot to himself, there is a nurse for every one or two persons, and he can now hope to recover.

XIII

The Return

Danny begins the homeward journey.[1] He is not alone. Dario is with him. They are part of a handful to leave Ebensee together. It is perhaps some three or four weeks after liberation. He is still in prison uniform; he is still quite a sight. Avitaminosis consumes his body and leaves its ugly imprint throughout. He is a fragile entity.

He boards a train, but he is very weak and ill. He sinks into his seat without reflecting on other trains in other places. He cannot speculate. Time and thought are in suspension. Is he in a torpor? Possibly. The wisdom of the body is limitless. If it occurs now, an assault of the truth of his predicament will kill him. It may kill him even unto this very day, and if in an unguarded moment he peers into the

---

1. On May 26, 1945, the Americans provided Danny with a provisional identity card as a civilian internee at Mauthausen. It covered the period from February 3, 1945, to May 6, 1945, and was issued from Mauthausen.

abyss inadvertently, he will flee the chasm within a milli-second. If it is a door, he shuts it; if it is a birth, he aborts it. He has lived in the flame long enough; he is as tempered as he can be. There is nothing more to anneal. The craft to forge the errant, molten tributaries of his *tristesse* does not exist.

Danny's first stop is in Bologna.[2] He remembers this. People are kind and gracious, direct and unaffected. There is food there, waiting for them at the train station, and they eat. He can speak Italian, and he can understand the Italian people well. He is comfortable, and he is relaxed. He allows things to happen; he allows them to be done for him. A sense of warmth, a sense of welcome enters. Before long, he will be in a boarding house on the outskirts of town.

For two days, he and the others will use the house as their home base, and it is here that additional certification arrives and is presented to him along with a change of clothes. It is here, too, that something new enters. The fellows, informed by some kindly soul as to the whereabouts of the local brothel, venture into town in pursuit . . . of what? One can hardly say. Was it carnal adventure? Or the idea of it? The presence of women? The look and fra-grance of them? The pleasure of it all? Did so much innocence remain after what they had been through? Yes. Yes, it did. Were they then still young? Still alive? Frivo-lous? Extraordinary. They had no means for the enterprise, and yet they were met with understanding. They were received with cordiality. And now, Danny knows nothing more of his companions. He is attracted to a girl who seems to like him, and he looks at her. It is really all he can do, and he does it. It is enough. It is a great deal, in fact.

2. It was June 26.

At the end of their stay, they once more board the train. They are on their way to Brindisi, the changeover point from where they will take a transport plane, a Dakota, to Athens. Some dozen or so former internees from the camps will be aboard, and Dario will be among them. Danny's prison garb is in a rucksack, which he carries, and on July 2, 1945, he will enter Athens in ordinary attire. And now, in Greece, Danny and Dario go their separate ways. Oh yes, they had known one another before the war, and they had been friendly, too, but the depth of their relationship is to season into something strong and indissoluble far from their native land and in the quiescence of time.

The contingent that alights and disperses on that day is not the first to have arrived from the camps. It has been preceded by a man by the name of Bati, a Sephardic Jew, whose arrival coincides with the approach of Passover.[3] "They must know," he thinks concerning the few who have survived in hiding, "but how can I spoil this holiday with such news as I have to tell?" Bati cannot do that. He cannot cast gloom upon a celebration so significant. "I shall wait," he decides. "I shall wait until it passes, and then I shall speak." But when the time comes and he speaks, he is not believed. "Bati is crazy," they think. "Bati is mad," they say. "He is deranged." And poor Bati, who is not believed, is put in an asylum, where he stays for something like two weeks. After that, news trickles in, and sometimes, like now, a few return.[4] The catastrophe has to be absorbed; it no longer can be deferred.

3. Bati, who came from Salonika, returned there. The account refers to that city, and not to Athens.

4. Ninety-six percent of the Jews of Salonika perished. Athens lost approximately one-third its Jewish population.

The Greeks at the station are very neutral, so neutral, in fact, that they are cold. They are indifferent, superficial, and bureaucratic. There is no reception to speak of, and it is not at all like Italy. He is processed like an object, and little more. In due time, he boards a bus.

Danny sets out to find the friend he loves above all others. There is no reason to believe he is alive, and none to believe he is at the Politikon Nosokomion, the community hospital in which he had been a surgeon, but this is where Danny begins. He makes his inquiry on arrival, learns that Dr. Benveniste is not in, leaves a note, and walks for the remainder of the day. In the evening, he returns to the Nosokomion. Daniel Benveniste is in, and the two friends meet at last. It is a reunion to remember.

Benveniste is Danny's senior by nine years; he is a friend, a brother, and a mentor.[5] Danny had come to know and ultimately admire Benveniste for his knowledge and the quality of his generosity and was especially indebted to him for having inspired his awakening in the sciences. When Benveniste came to Salonika on seasonal breaks from the university he attended in Padua, the two got together—and one Daniel taught the other the principles and intricacies of what he had learned. In brief, Benveniste's enthusiasm inspired Danny and spurred him on. It led him to take an abiding interest in the nature of things, and it perfected in him a keen reserve about our ordinary assumptions or perceptions.

Now that they are together, they closet themselves. Yes, literally. They secret themselves in a tiny bit of a room, and

5. Danny met Benveniste through Senor, a younger brother, who was his friend. Senor was killed in a concentration camp early in the war.

soon they are joined by Dr. George Avlamis, a non-Jew who not only served in the Underground but also served as the chief of all the partisan units in the area, a man to whom Benveniste owed his life. They begin to drink wine and tell tales, but Danny, who has eaten little or nothing, gets very drunk indeed. Benveniste's story loops through the chinks between inebriation and sobriety. In honor of the occasion, neither Benveniste nor Avlamis is quite sober, either, but the following story emerges:

Perhaps there is an act of sabotage and perhaps there is a killing of a German soldier—one does not always learn the rationale for such things—but one day, the SS round up fifty Greek hostages for execution. They target a specific area and cordon it off in order to maximize terror and facilitate the entrapment of the prey, and then they pounce. Benveniste and forty-five others are caught and crated onto a truck, destined to die, but Benveniste flees, or, at least, tries to escape. In so doing, he breaks his leg and is recaptured easily. But now, instead of shooting him, the Germans bring him to the Nosokomion to have the fracture tended to; there he must mend before being shot. What is more, he is to die as a Greek and not as a Jew, for none suspects his origins. *En fin,* since German guards are posted at his door, it remains for Dr. Avlamis to manufacture a ruse to require their presence elsewhere, and such is the case. A plan is devised, an escape is effected, and Benveniste remains in hiding until the end of the war. . . .

Danny sleeps the night away in the little room, and in the morning, he roams the streets. When it grows dark, he returns. For perhaps three days, he observes this pattern, and then he seeks out Mary Rouben, whom he has known for as long as he can remember. He climbs the stairs to her

apartment, knocks on the door, and stays to both con-
valesce and integrate such strands of his life as yet remain.

After a few months, he and Benveniste decide to rent a
room of their own. With little or no funds, this is not easy
to achieve, but in time they find a place they can share in
the Kassariani District. They are now in a suburb of Athens
and in a home that has no running water, but it scarcely
matters. The nearest water supply is about a mile away;
they resort to the public bathhouse and take the half-hour
bus ride into Athens within stride. Primitive or not, friends
come to visit, and one night, as many as eighteen persons
sleep in their room. During this period, his closeness to
Mary remains a constant; he sees her often and often stays
with her and her family, so that, in effect, he has two homes.

Each morning for the next six months or so, Danny
accompanies Benveniste to the hospital, where he is introduced as a colleague. He is present in the wards, and he is
present during surgery; he learns from everything and
everyone. Appropriately dressed for the part, enterprising
in imagination and improvisation, intelligent and humorous,
they pull it off. Soon enough, however, Benveniste sees that
something idiosyncratic arises each time they have lunch
together in one or another street café. Unable to restrain
himself any longer, he asks Danny what he is doing—for,
wherever they go, Danny picks up a piece of bread, tucks it
into the tiny pocket in the front of his trousers, and then
taps his fingers over it reassuringly. "I'll never be without
bread," Danny replies.

Salonika is destroyed, and the ashes are strewn within.
Danny is their receptacle, even as he is the living limb of an
uprooted tree. We do not mix metaphors; reason has gone
awry. Never more will he see his enraptured father at the

Victrola, listening to Caruso, and never more will he see his mother attempt to outwit the dark chambers of death with all the light in her power. Unfinished lives live in wisps of imagination; that is the land they inhabit. They speak in the winds of memory; they touch like mist.

Danny has had a marvelous interlude with Benveniste at the hospital, but he must move on. The legs that have carried him so far will have to carry him farther. It is time to take the next step, and so one day Danny gets a job with the Joint Distribution Committee, feeding and clothing displaced persons. He is twenty-two years old when he meets the love of his life while working there.

Epilogue

We meet to clarify minor details and begin to go over the schema of Auschwitz-Birkenau. Danny, who knows little or nothing about Auschwitz I from personal experience, merely glances at the material pertaining to that facility. It is clear that he is interested, and it is equally clear that he will familiarize himself with the data later on, but for now, it is Auschwitz II, or Birkenau, that absorbs him wholly. A unique orientation takes place. "I want to learn," says Danny. "I want to know what happened to me." And so we locate the women's camp (BI), and we locate the men's camp (BII). We find Lager D, Block 13, and approximate the lager kitchens nearby; we find the family camp, and we find BIIb, tracing the path along which Jenny and he shared furtive glimpses of one another. Canada, the sauna, the woods, and the pits are recognized, as is Bunker 1. But Bunker 2, or 5, as it was later numbered, constitutes new information, as does the existence of BIII.

For a moment, Danny leans back in his swivel chair. "I

know why I don't remember," he says. "I don't remember because I never thought I would live; it was inconceivable to me that somehow I would survive.

"If I had to do it all over again, I would try. I would try, because I am convinced that it can happen again. I have come to believe that everyone is capable of committing the most appalling crimes, and that it is useless to think someone else is the monster. We have this capacity, too."

He has seen the slaughter of the innocent, and he has seen what a relentless system provokes in evil residue, but I have heard him speak of other things and other men. "There are those amongst us who can and do remain incorruptible, even within the framework of an Auschwitz," I say. "That is true," he replies, "but they are very few."

Glossary

Alle Antreten. Command for everyone to line up.

Andartis, pl. *Andartes.* Rebel in the Greek Underground.

Appell. Roll call of concentration camp prisoners.

Ashkenazi, pl. *Ashkenazim.* An Eastern European Yiddish-speaking Jew or his descendant.

Blockälteste. Block elder and inmate functionary in charge of a single concentration camp barracks.

Blocksperre. The locking of barracks' doors at night and during special selections.

Canada. A complex of some thirty huts at the west end of Birkenau, where the belongings of newly arrived prisoners were sorted and stored by the SS. Like the country of Canada, it symbolized a place of great riches.

Gestapo. Geheime Staatspolizei or Secret State Police; a symbol of the Nazi reign of terror.

Hauptscharführer. SS master sergeant.

Heizer. Stoker or boilerman.

Kapo. Prisoner of a concentration camp in charge of a working party. An inmate functionary.

Kommando. Labor or work detail.

Ladino. Judeo-Spanish. The language of the Sephardim, whose roots stem from pre-Inquisition Spain.

Meister. Master or boss.

Mexico. Compound BIII at Auschwitz-Birkenau, where approximately 15,000 Hungarian Jewish women were housed in unfinished barracks. Their colorful, incongruous clothing provided the origins for this ironic term.

Müllbrenner. A place where garbage is burned.

Musulman. A prisoner who has stopped fighting for survival. The emaciated, walking "dead."

Ntou. Movement, attack, revolt. Greek slang.

Oberscharführer. SS technical sergeant.

Organizing. Generic term in prisoner usage in the camps, meaning to steal, filch, or appropriate something, usually food, clothing, cigarettes, etc.

Politische Abteilung. Where the various departments of the camp Gestapo were housed in the main camp of Auschwitz I. An inquisitional organization that spied on prisoners, civilian employees, and SS alike and investigated escapes and conspiracies. They took their directives from both the camp commandant and the Gestapo.

Schreiber. Inmate clerks who assisted the roll call leader and supervised the preparation of all reports and orders. Such clerks also served in the labor brigades, the inmate infirmary, and various SS offices.

Selection. Euphemism for the process of choosing victims for the gas chambers whenever a new transport arrived in the Nazi camps, by separating them from those fit to work. An on-going process in the camps.

Sephardi, pl. *Sephardim.* A Jew who can trace his roots to pre-Inquisition Spain.

Sonderkommando. Special work detail. The prisoner or prisoners who were assigned to this detail were slave laborers; they worked in the gas chambers and crematoria at Auschwitz-Birkenau.

SS. Abbreviation. Usually written with two runic lightning symbols, which are indicators for the *Schutzstaffel,* or Protective Units. The Nazi paramilitary; the black-shirted storm troops built into a gigantic empire by Heinrich Himmler, which included the police, the camp guards, and the SS fighting units (Waffen SS).

Stücke. A thing, object, or item.

Unterscharführer. SS sergeant.

Volksdeutscher. Ethnic German. A German of foreign nationality.

Vorarbeiter. A prisoner foreman.

Appendix

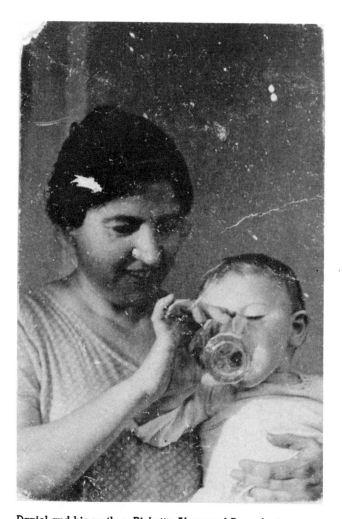

Daniel and his mother, *Ricketta Abravanel Bennahmias*
This is one of two existing photos of Danny's mother to have
survived the war and was given to him by a friend after his
return. The original is a sepia-tinted scrap, scarcely larger than
an inch by an inch and a half.
Salonika, c. 1923

Transports from Greece

Numerical Summary of Greek Jews Deported, Placed in Camp, and Killed in Auschwitz*

Sequential number	Date of arrival	From	Number deported	Numbers assigned to men directed to camp	Number of those men	Numbers of women assigned to camp	Number of those women	Total number of men and women	Number killed in gas chambers
1	2	3	4	5	6	7	8	9	10
1	20.3.43 r.	Saloniki	2800	109371—109787	417	38721—38912	192	609	2191
2	24.3.43 r.	Saloniki	2800	109896—110479	584	38962—39191	230	814	1986
3	25.3.43 r.	Saloniki	1901	110483—110941	459	39193—39428	236	695	1206
4	30.3.43 r.	Saloniki	2501	111147—111458	312	39623—39763	141	453	2048
5	3.4.43 r.	Saloniki	2800	112307—112640	334	39964—40221	258	592	2208
6	9.4.43 r.	Saloniki	2500	112974—113291	318	40280—40440	161	479	2021
7	10.4.43 r.	Saloniki	2750	114094—114630	537	40537—40782	246	783	1967
8	13.4.43 r.	Saloniki	2800	114875—115374	500	40841—41204	364	864	1936
9	17.4.43 r.	Saloniki	3000	115848—116314	467	41354—41615	262	729	2271
10	18.4.43 r.	Saloniki	2501	116317—116676	360	41616—41860	245	605	1896
11	22.4.43 r.	Saloniki	2800	117199—117453	255	42038—42450	413	668	3132
12	26.4.43 r.	Saloniki	2700	118425—118869	445	42882—43074	193	638	2062
13	28.4.43 r.	Saloniki	3070	118888—119067	180	43123—43483	361	541	2529
14	4.5.43 r.	Saloniki	2930	119781—120090	220	43779—44096	318	538	2392
15	7.5.43 r.	Saloniki	1000	—	—	44259—44326	68	68	932
16	8.5.43 r.	Saloniki	2500	120650—121217	568	44380—44626	247	815	1685
17	16.5.43 r.	Saloniki	4500	121910—122375	466	44934—45144	211	677	3823

18	8.6.43 r.	Saloniki	880	124325—124544	220	45995—46082	88	308	572
19	18.8.43 r.	Saloniki	1800	136919—137189	271	—	—	271	1529
20	11.4.44 r.	Ateny	1500	182440—182789	320	numbers unknown	113	433	1067
21	30.6.44 r.	Ateny i Korfu	2000	A15229—A15674	446	A8282—A8412	131	577	1423
22	16.8.44 r.	wyspa Rodos	2500	B7159—B7504	346	A24215—A24468	254	600	1900
		Lacznie	54533		8025		4732	12757	41776

* Worksheet arrived at by the authors on the basis of railroad tickets, numerical indications of prison transports, lists of the quarantined in the men's camp KL Auschwitz 2 (Birkenau) upon confrontation of personal sheets of prisoners, indications of women prisoners chosen on August 21, 1943, for death in the gas chamber.

Danny and his friends and family arrived on the twentieth transport.

+Original in Auschwitz; photocopy with Magnes Museum in Berkeley, California.
Translated from Polish

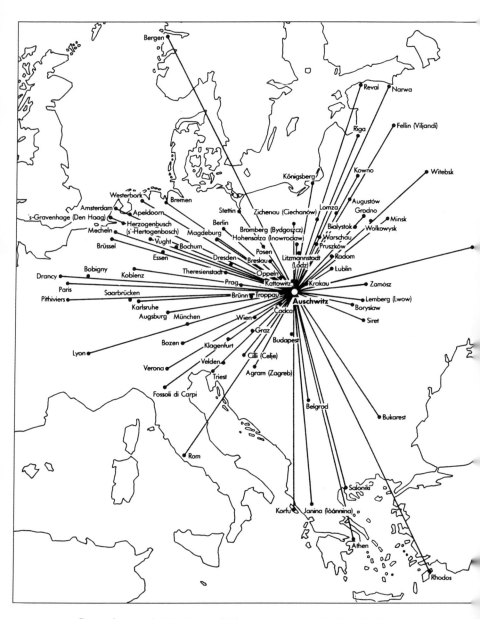

General map of cities from which transports went to Auschwitz.

Tracks from Auschwitz to Birkenau

Photo: S. Camhi

Auschwitz

Photo: Courtesy of Ira Nowinski

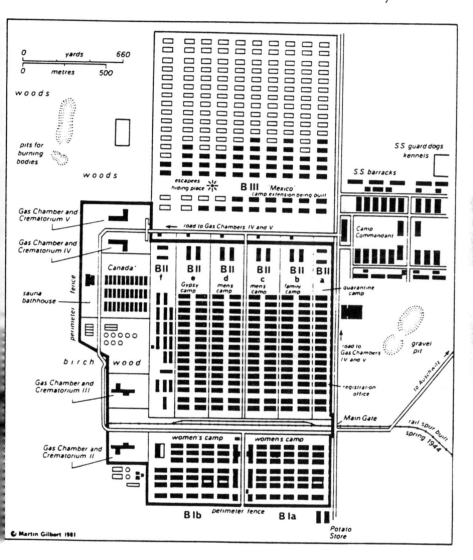

Auschwitz II—Birkenau

Rendition by Martin Gilbert, depicting Crematoria II, III, IV, and V
Auschwitz and the Allies, p. 195. Permission of Martin Gilbert

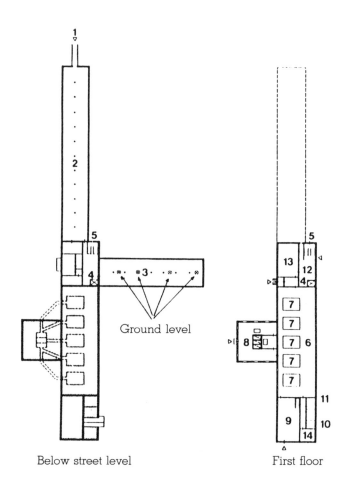

Ground level

Below street level   First floor

Crematoria II and I in this account. (Each a mirror image of the other.)

Crematoria II and I in this account. (Each a mirror image of the other.)
1 Stairs to changing room; 2 Changing room; 3 Gas chamber; ■ concrete pillar; ⊗ gas inlet; 4 Lift for corpses; 5 Chute for remains of corpses; 6 Incineration room; 7 Ovens, each with 3 chambers; 8 Chimney; 9 Coke store; 10 Washroom WC; 11 *Kommandoführer's* office; 12 Execution room; 13 Room where gold fillings melted down in crematorium 1, dissecting room; 14 In crematorium 2, quarters of those who melted down gold fillings

We assume the dotted rectangles represent the placement of the ventilators.

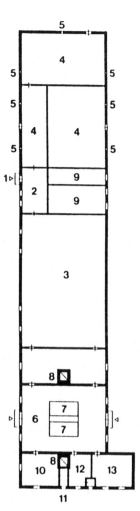

Crematoria IV and III in this account. (Each a mirror image of the other.) *Note the absence of ventilators.*

Crematoria IV and III in this account. (Each a mirror image of the other.) *Note the absence of ventilators.*

1 Entrance to the changing room; 2 Ante-room; 3 Changing room; Execution room; Corpse room; In crematorium 3 from summer 1944 the *Sonderkommando's* quarters; 4 Gas chamber; 5 Gas inlet; 6 Incineration room; 7 Oven with 4 incineration chambers; 8 Chimney; 9 *Sonderkommando's* quarters. In crematorium 4 from autumn 1944 quarters of the *Sonderkommando;* 10 *Kommandoführer's* office; 11 *Kapos'* headquarters; 12 Washroom/WC; 13 Coke store

Adapted from Müller: Eyewitness Auschwitz.

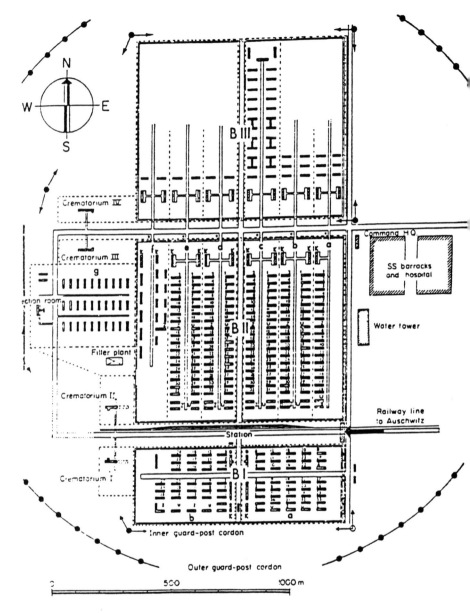

Auschwitz II——Birkenau

B1 was the women's compound. BII was the men's compound, and BIII, known as *Mexico*, was never finished. Section BIIb later became part of the women's camp. Canada is designated by BIIg.

Rendition by Erich Eulka, depicting Crematoria I, II, III, and IV

Cannister of Zyklon B gas
Photo: Courtesy of Ira Nowinski

Birkenau

On January 20, 1945—two days after the death marches began—the SS blew up the already largely dismantled Crematoria I and II *(refer to Kulka's schema)*. In the photo above are the ruins of Crematorium II.

Photo: Courtesy of Ira Nowinski

Ebensee, Austria. May 7, 1945

Survivors of Ebensee concentration camp prepare to be evacuated.
National Archives

Ebensee, Austria, May 8, 1945

Members of F Co., 3rd Squadron, Mechanized of 3rd Cavalry Group, overran the large and brutal Nazi prison camp in Ebensee, Austria, and liberated about 16,000 prisoners of 25 different nationalities, all in various stages of starvation. They were nourished with good food, given medical care, and, when stronger, would be evacuated. Here, heaps of clothing belonging to the prisoners are being sorted out for fumigation by some of the stronger liberated prisoners. Some 60,000 in all were freed from Mauthausen and its satellites.

National Archives

After the bulldozers, a tent city for the sick . . .

Three days after the Americans arrived, Danny was housed in the largest tent with about forty others. Here he received true medical attention. The Auslander section, POW Camp #2. Ebensee, Austria.

National Archives. Photo released by field press censor, September 6, 1945

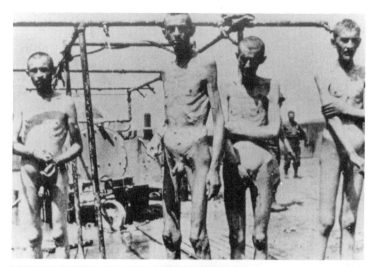

Free at last . . .

Photo from the collection of the *Ebenseer Fotoklub* in Ebensee, Austria, presently in the archives of the Holocaust Library in San Francisco **(top)**

Danny surmises this may have been potato peel soup, an unheard of luxury for the former slave laborers who devoured grass, leaves, brown coal, wood, and bone if and when they could.

Prisoners who would have killed for a piece of bread prior to liberation, scaled down their intake of wholesome food in order to survive. Photo from the collection of the *Ebenseer Fotoklub* in Ebensee, Austria, presently in the archives of the Holocaust Library in San Francisco. **(bottom)**

Danny was somewhere to the right of the entryway.

The infirmary where Danny stayed was near the crematorium for "quick" disposal of the dead. Relaxed stance of the prisoners indicates the liberation of the camp had taken place. *(Note seated figure.)* Photo from the collection of the *Ebenseer Fotoklub* in Ebensee, Austria, presently in the archives of the Holocaust Library in San Francisco.

Americans provide aid and comfort to a dying former slave, whose system rebels at the sudden introduction of food.

Photo from the collection of the *Ebenseer Fotoklub* of Ebensee, Austria, presently in the archives of the Holocaust Library in San Francisco

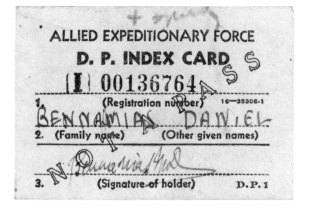

BUONO PRELEVAMENTO VIVERI

N° 64

Name

N° in Family 5.

Monīh

	1	2	3	4	5	6	7	8	9	10	11
V I V E R I	12	13	14	15	16	17	18	19	20	21	22
	23	24	25	26	27	28	29	30	31	CUCINA	

BOLOGNA CITY

A. M. G. TRANSIT CENTRE FOR REFUGEES
DISPLACED PERSONS & REPATRIATION SUB-COMMISSION
ALLIED COMMISSION

N° 64	N° in family	N° of room

Name *Benzanmas Daniele*

Age *1923*

Arrived 26.6 From *Justria*

Departed _____ For *Roma*

Remarks

✝
ΕΛΛΗΝΙΚΟΣ ΕΡΥΘΡΟΣ ΣΤΑΥΡΟΣ
ΓΡΑΦΕΙΟΝ ΑΙΧΜΑΛΩΤΩΝ
Όδὸς Κόλοκοτρώνη 1— ΑΘΗΝΑΙ

ΒΕΒΑΙΩΣΙΣ

Τὸ Γραφεῖον Αἰχμαλώτων τοῦ Ἑλληνικοῦ Ἐρυθροῦ Σταυροῦ πιστοποιεῖ
ὅτι ὡς προκύπτει ἐκ τῶν εἰς χεῖρας του στοιχείων ὁ ....
................................διετέλεσε πολιτικὸς κρατούμενος τῶν Γερμανι-
κῶν Ἀρχῶν Κατοχῆς εἰς ....καὶ ἀπελευθερωθεὶς ἐπα-
νῆλθεν εἰς Ἀθήνας τὴν ....1945..........

Ἀθῆναι τῇ ..... Ἰουλίου 1946

Διὰ τὸ Γραφεῖον Αἰχμαλώτων τοῦ Ε.Ε.Σ.

Bologna City and certificate. This last certificate was issued in 1946 by the
Greek mission of the displaced persons' division of UNRRA.

A.E.F. D.P. REGISTRATION RECORD

(1) Registration No. **4001367614**

Original ☑ Duplicate ☐

For coding purposes: A. B. C. D. E. F. G. H. I. J.

(2) Family Name	Other Given Names	(3) Sex	(4) Marital Status	(5) Claimed Nationality
BENNAMIAS	DANIEL	M. ☑	Single ☑ Married ☐ F. ☐ Widowed ☐ Divorced ☐	GREEK

(6) Birthdate	Birthplace	Province	Country	(7) Religion (Optional)	(8) Number of Accompanying Family Members:
16-6-1923	SALONIQUE	SALONIQUE	GREECE	Jew	

(9) Number of Dependents: **1**

(10) Full Name of Father: **BENNAMIAS MARCO**

(11) Full Maiden Name of Mother: **ABRAVANEL RICHETTA**

(12) Desired Destination			(13) Last Permanent Residence or Residence January 1, 1938.		
City or Village	Province	Country	City or Village	Province	Country
ATHENS		GREECE	SALONIQUE		GREECE

(14) Usual Trade, Occupation or Profession: **STUDENT**

(15) Performed in What Kind of Establishment:

(16) Other Trades or Occupations:

(17) Languages Spoken in Order of Fluency: **ENGLISH GREEK FRENCH ITAL. SPAG.**

(18) Do You Claim to be a Prisoner of War: Yes ☐ No ☑

(19) Amount and Kind of Currency in your Possession:

(20) Signature of Registrant: *Bennamias D.*

(21) Signature of Registrar: *Stella*

Date: **1 VII 1945**

Assembly Center No. **I.T.31**

(22) Destination or Reception Center:

(23) Code for Issue	Name or Number												City or Village							Province					Country		
	1	2	3	4	5	6	7	8	9	10	11	12	13	14	15	16	17	18	19	20	21	22	23	24	25	26	27	28

(24) Remarks

DP-2
10—39781-1

MEDICAL CLEARANCE CERTIFICATE

(31) SUPPLEMENTARY RECORD

(25) Dates of Disinfestation — 1st / 2nd
Types: D.D.T. / AL.63 M.K.² / HEAT / O

Temporary identity certificate issued—:

	Number	Date	Signature of Authority

(26) Physical Condition on Arrival

L.	M.	C. D.	D.

Remarks

(27) Immunization Record

Type	Dose	Date	Init.
T. (Epid)	1.		
	2.		
	3.		
D.	1.		
	2.		
T. T. (Tab.)	1.		
	2.		
	3.		
O.			

S. Vacc. Read.	Date	Initials	Reaction L. V.

Arrival Medical Inspection —: Date

Medical Examiner

(28) Final Medical Inspection —: Date M.

Medical Examiner

(29) Movement Authorization or Visa

(30) Reception Center Record

10—39781-1 U. S. GOVERNMENT PRINTING OFFICE

Danny, to the left, with two acquaintances
Photo, taken by a friend two days after Danny's arrival in Greece, coincides with the interval he stayed with Benveniste at the *Nosokomion*. Athens, July 4, 1945.

Dario Gabbai as he
appeared in 1951.
Los Angeles, California

Dr. Daniel Benveniste
as he appeared in the
late sixties, early seventies.

Unofficial Translation of Letters from Auschwitz.
(All originals and copies of correspondence are in author's possession.)

I-8523/108/3225/87   Oswiecim, November 27, 1987

Dear Mrs Fromer,
    As Mr Erich Kulka has informed our state Auschwitz Museum you are in
direct contacts with former Auschwitz prisoners and members of Sonderkommando Daniel Bennahmias and Dario Gabai.
    In connection with our current research works we are interested in
obtaining their memoires related to their stay in Auschwitz and a work in
Sonderkommando as well as the other materials/photographs, documents,
souvenirs/.
    If you have got such memoires or materials Museum would like you send
their copies. We can offer you for them our books in exchange.
    Museum would like receive the addresses of the above mentioned persons
too.

                                        Yours sincerely
                                        DIRECTOR
                                        MA Kazimierz Smolen

Dear Madam,
    The State Museum Auschwitz thanks you very much for your letter of April
29, 1988 and your readiness of helping us in gaining of memoirs of former
Auschwitz-Birkenau and members of Sonderkommando prisoners Daniel
Bennahmias and Dario Gabbai.
    Museum would like to explain that because of destruction of the most of
Auschwitz records only memoirs and relations of former prisoner enable us to
reconstruct the camp history. Therefore Museum, whose purpose is between
other a reconstruction of the camp history, collects over and over again such
kind of historical resources. They are now about 2500 in number preserved in
our archives and used for searching works. Especially worthy are memoirs and
relations of former prisoners, who were employed in crematoria and gas
chambers, as the nearest eyewitnesses of mass extermination. Out of about
2000 prisoners who served any time in Sonderkommando only severals scores
survived the war because of it every memoir of former member of Sonderkommando is very valuable in particular now when the existence of gas chambers
and crematoria is questioned. There are reasons Museum would be grateful for
any help in obtaining of memoirs of above mentioned former prisoners.

Once more thereafter Museum asks you for transmission of the request to them or to give us their addresses in order to write to them directly. Also in the latter case any your recommendation would be desirable.

Yours sincerely
DIRECTOR
MA Kazimierz Smolen

Letter of 13 lipiec, 1989, *Oswieçim-Brzezinka, dn.*

I-8523/74/2353/89

Dear Madam,

State Museum in Oswiecim (Auschwitz) confirms receipt of letter dated December 6, 1988. (Museum received it on July 6, 1989.) The Museum gratefully thanks for addresses of D. Gabbai and D. Bennahmias sent to us. The Museum informs that it has not received until now your work (essays) which you intended to send in December of the past year.

Respectfully,
Kazimierz Smolen
Director

Letter of 23 IV, 1990, *Oswieçim-Brzezinka, dn.*

Dear Madam,

State Museum in Oswiecim confirms receipt and thanks for sending the second half of memoirs of Daniel Bennahmias, which you worked out. It was transferred to the collection of the local archives, section "Recollections."

At the same time the Museum requests that you forward the camp number of Daniel Bennahmias, since same is not given in the memoirs.

Hoping that we can count on further cooperation, I enclose my respect and appreciation.

Kazimierz Smolen
Director

Select Bibliography

Abzug, Robert H. *Americans and the Liberation of Nazi Concentration Camps.* New York and Oxford: Oxford University Press, 1985.

Czech, Danuta. *Auschwitz.* Warsaw: Interpress Publishers, 1978.

——. *Kalendarium: Der Ereignisse im Konzentrationslager Auschwitz-Birkenau 1939–1945.* Reinbek bei Hamburg: Rowohlt Press, 1989.

Feig, Konnilyn G. *Hitler's Death Camps: The Sanity of Madness.* New York: Holmes and Meier, 1970.

Freund, Florian. *Das Konzentrationslager Ebensee und Die Raketenrüstung.* Vienna: Verlag Gesellschaftskritik G.m.b.H., 1989.

Friedlander, Henry, and Sybil Milton, eds. *The Holocaust: Ideology, Bureaucracy, and Genocide.* New York: Kraus International Publications, 1980.

Gilbert, Martin. *Atlas of the Holocaust.* Jerusalem, Tel Aviv, Haifa: Steimatsky's Agency, 1982.

——. *Auschwitz and the Allies.* New York: Holt, Rinehart, and Winston, 1981.

————. *The Holocaust: A History of the Jews of Europe during the Second World War.* New York: Holt, Rinehart, and Winston, 1985.

Hart, Kitty. *Return to Auschwitz.* New York: Atheneum, 1982.

Hellman, Peter. *The Auschwitz Album: A Book Based upon an Album Discovered by a Concentration Camp Survivor, Lili Meier.* New York: Random House, 1981.

Hilberg, Raul. *The Destruction of the European Jews.* New York and London: Holmes and Meier, 1985.

Kantor, Alfred. *The Book of Alfred Kantor.* New York: McGraw-Hill, 1971.

Katris, John A. *Eyewitness in Greece: The Colonels Come to Power.* St. Louis: New Critics Press, 1971.

Levi, Primo. *Survival in Auschwitz.* London: Collier Macmillan, 1959.

Müller, Filip. *Eyewitness Auschwitz.* New York: Stein and Day, 1979.

Nahon, Marco. *Birkenau, The Camp of Death.* Tuscaloosa and London: University of Alabama Press, 1989.

Naumann, Bernd. *Auschwitz.* New York: Frederick A. Praeger, 1966.

Piper, Franciszek. "Extermination," in *Auschwitz.* Warsaw: Interpress Publishing, 1978.

Index

About the Authors

*R*ebecca Camhi Fromer is co-founder of the Judah L. Magnes Museum and a writer in Berkeley, California.

*S*teven B. Bowman is Professor and Acting Director of Judaic Studies, University of Cincinnati.